All right, but how do you build predictive models in a responsible way? This is a question I am often asked by data scientists at different levels of experience. Seemingly simple but at the same time challenging because there are several orthogonal threads and perspectives of different stakeholders that should be addressed.

Model developers focus on automation of model training, monitoring of performance, debugging, and other MLOps-related matters. Users of predictive models are more interested in explainability, transparency and security, while fairness, bias, ethics are issues of interest to society. Regulators are interested in the consequences of model deployments, especially those with large-scale impacts.

Taking these perspectives into account we focus on three essential elements related to Responsible Machine Learning (RML).

Algorithms - Often, to capture complex relationships in data, you need to use advanced and elastic machine learning algorithms. These, however, should not be used without understanding how they work. So a discussion about responsible modelling must touch on the topic of how complex models work.

Software - Training of advanced models is a computationally demanding process. The libraries that allow for efficient training are low-level engineering masterpieces. Professionals use good tools, so a story about responsible modelling must include a section related to good software.

Process - Predictive modelling is not only about tools but also about planning, logistics, communication, deadlines and objectives. The process of data and model exploration is iterative, as in each iteration, we head towards better and better models. Knowing the tools does not help much if you do not know when and how to use them. Therefore, to talk about responsible modelling, we need to talk about the processes behind modelling.

This book is a unique entanglement of all these aspects together at the same time. You will find here selected modern machine learning techniques and the intuition behind them. Methods are supplemented by code snippets with examples in R language[1]. The process is shown through a comic book describing the adventures of two characters, Beta and Bit. The interaction of these two shows the decisions that analysts often face, whether to try a different model, try another technique for exploration or look for other data — questions like: how to compare models or how to validate them.

[1] R Core Team. *R: A Language and Environment for Statistical Computing*. R Foundation for Statistical Computing, Vienna, Austria, 2021. URL https://www.R-project.org/

Model development is responsible and challenging work but also an exciting adventure. Sometimes textbooks focus only on the technical side, losing all the fun. Here we are going to have it all.

Przemysław Biecek
Warszawa, 2022

SOMEWHERE IN WARSAW.
IN A BUILDING AT WARSAW UNIVERSITY OF TECHNOLOGY. THE SECRET HQS OF MI2DataLab.
MI DATA LAB
BIT IS COMPLETELY WRAPPED UP IN PROGRAMMING AI THAT PLAYS TETRIS FOR HIM.

MESSAGE
MESSAGE
FROM   : MR. MI2
TO   : BETA AND BIT
SUBJECT : NEW TASK
BODY   : TOP PRIORITY!
OUR FIELD AGENTS ARE OPERATING IN AN AREA WHERE THE SARS-COV-2
VIRUS HAS BEEN IDENTIFIED. WE URGENTLY NEED A MODEL TO ASSESS
THE RISK OF DEATH IN CASE OF INFECTION. WE NEED TO KNOW IN WHAT
ORDER THEY SHOULD BE VACCINATED.
YOU HAVE 6 HOURS!

Predictive models have been used throughout entire human history. Priests in ancient Egypt could predict when the Nile would flood or a solar eclipse would come. Developments in statistics, increasing availability of datasets, and increasing computing power allow predictive models to be built faster and deployed in a rapidly growing number of applications.

Today, predictive models are used virtually everywhere. Planning of the supply chain for a large corporation, recommending lunch or a movie for the evening, or predicting traffic jams in a city. Newspapers are full of exciting applications.

But how are such predictive models developed?

On the following pages, we go through a life cycle of an example predictive model[2] from the concept phase, through design, training, checking, to the deployment. We present an agile approach to building and exploring Machine Learning (ML) models, inspired by the agile approach to software development[3]. The main principles of Agile ML are: continuous adaptation to newly acquired knowledge, continuous prototyping of the solution, dynamic planning, and effective communication. The life cycle of a predictive model is summarized by the diagram below.

[2] We use an example actually built on real data to predict the risk of severe Covid disease progression. But the approach presented can be applied to a very broad class of problems.

[3] Agile manifesto https://en.wikipedia.org/wiki/Agile_software_development

Figure 1: Developing a predictive model often involves many iterations. In this book too, iteration by iteration, we build increasingly complex models, compare them against others, and extract useful information through various Explanatory Model Analysis (EMA) techniques.

Subsequent iterations consist of exploration of literature, data and models, assembly of new solutions and validation after validation. But in addition to these steps, we also show the concept phase, in which the problem to be solved is specified, and the deployment phase, in which the final model is delivered to the users.

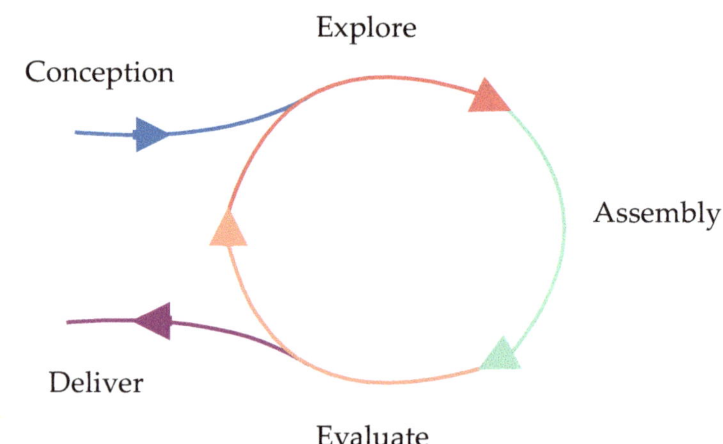

We present the life cycle of model development and validation using an example of a binary classification model. We start with a simple model derived from domain knowledge and expand it into a fully data-driven random forest model with automatically tuned hyperparameters. The description of the methods is supplemented with code snippets that you can use to replicate all the presented results yourself. It's worth playing around with these codes to understand better how the described methods work.

Due to the limited space, the descriptions of the methods of both machine learning algorithms and explainable artificial intelligence are brief. If you want to learn more about predictive modelling, I highly recommend the book *An Introduction to Statistical Learning* (ISL)[4]. For those interested in a more detailed description of Explanatory Model Analysis (EMA) and eXplainable Artificial Intelligence (XAI), you will find much more in the book *Explanatory Model Ana-*

[4] Gareth James, Daniela Witten, Trevor Hastie, and Robert Tibshirani. *An Introduction to Statistical Learning: with Applications in R.* Springer, 2013. URL https://www.statlearning.com/

lysis[5]. Both are available in paperback but can also be read free of charge in an electronic form.

The modelling approach presented in this book is inspired by the paper *Statistical modeling: the two cultures* by Leo Breiman[6]. It presents two views of modelling, one focused on building models that reflects the laws of nature and the other describing models focused on the effectiveness of predicting a certain trait. As we will show in this book, a bridge can be built between these two approaches. Effective models can and should be used to extract knowledge about a domain, and such knowledge can be furthered transformed into even more effective models.

[5] Przemyslaw Biecek and Tomasz Burzykowski. *Explanatory Model Analysis*. Chapman and Hall/CRC, New York, 2021. URL `https://pbiecek.github.io/ema/`

[6] Leo Breiman. Statistical modeling: the two cultures. *Statistical Science*, 16(3):199–231, 2001b

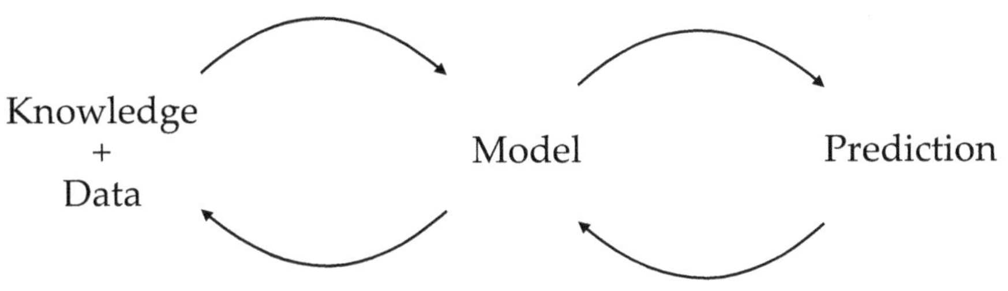

Figure 2: The first part of this book is devoted to the transformation of knowledge and data into a model and then into predictions. The second part of this book discusses how to learn from predictions, how the model works and how to extract information about the domain from the predictive model.

Another interesting point made by Leo Breiman in the article mentioned above is the Rashomon perspective for predictive modelling, i.e. situation in which several equally good models describe the same phenomenon differently. In this book, we show how to examine what different models say about the data. We introduce a pyramid for model exploration that forms a language in which we can show and cross-compare stories learned by different predictive models.

SARS-COV-2 case study

To demonstrate what responsible predictive modelling looks like, we used data obtained in collaboration with the Polish Institute of Hygiene in modelling mortality after the Covid infection. We realize that data on Coronavirus disease can evoke negative feelings. However, it is a good example of how predictive modelling can directly impact our society and how data analysis allows us to deal with complex, important and topical problems.

All the results presented in this book can be independently reproduced using the snippets and instructions presented in this book. If you do not want to retype them, then all the examples, data, and codes can be found on the webpage of this book[7]. Please note that the data presented at this URL is artificially generated to mirror relations in the actual data. But it does not contain real patients data.

[7] `https://betaandbit.github.io/RML/`

The procedure outlined here is presented for mortality modelling, but the same process can be replicated whether modelling patient survival, housing pricing, or credit scoring is concerned.

I'LL ASK MY BIOLOGIST AND DOCTOR FRIEND!
I'LL WRITE A SCRIPT SEARCHING FOR DATA ON THE NET.
I'LL LOOK FOR DATA ABOUT OTHER DISEASES.
I'LL USE BOT-NET TO CHAT WITH RESEARCHERS ALL OVER THE WORLD.
I'LL GO THROUGH SCIENTIFIC MAGAZINES!
SCIENTIFIC AMERICAN
THE CORONAVIRUS PANDEMIC
ATARI
I'LL SCRAPE DATA FROM INTERNET FORUMS.

Oh! Look what I've found!
Let's check it on the large screen.
We may use the stats to estimate the risk. Case closed!
Hang on a sec... I wonder how good this model will be.
1H

Hello model!

When browsing through examples of predictive modelling, one may get the wrong impression that the life cycle of the model begins with the data from the internet and ends with validation on an independent dataset. However, this is an oversimplification.

As you will see in a minute, we can create a model without raw data.

The life cycle of a predictive model begins with a **well-defined problem**. In this example, we are looking for a model that assesses the risk of death after being diagnosed with Covid. We don't want to guess who will survive and who won't. Instead, we want to construct a score that allows us to sort patients by their individual risk. Why do we need such a model? For example, those at higher risk of death could be given higher protection, such as providing them with pulse oximeters or preferential vaccination. For this reason, in the following sections, we introduce and use model performance measures that evaluate rankings of scores, such as Area Under Curve (AUC). Pick a model evaluation measure suitable for the problem posed.

Having defined the problem we want to solve, we can move to the next step, which is to **collect all the available information**. Often the solution to the problem can be found in the literature, whether in the form of a ready-made feature prediction function, a discussion of what features are important, or sample data.

If there are no ready-to-use solutions and we have to collect the data ourselves, it is always worth considering where and what data to collect in order to build the model on a **representative sample**[8]. The problem of data representativeness is a topic for a separate book. Incorrectly collected data will create biases that are hard to discover and even harder to fix.

[8] In our study, we used data on all patients reached by the sanitary inspectorate between March and August 2020. It would seem that data collected in this way would be free of bias, but we were able to detect some. In April, the pandemic spread faster among coal mine workers, who were more likely to be young men, which may have influenced the fluctuations in mortality.

We think of a predictive model as a function that computes certain predictions for specific input data. Usually, such a function is built automatically based on the data. But technically, the model can be any function defined in any way.

Our first model will be based on the statistics collected by the Centers for Disease Control and Prevention (CDC)[9]. That's right; sometimes, we don't need raw data to build a predictive model. We'll start by turning a table with mortality statistics into a model.

[9] https://www.cdc.gov/

Figure 3: Mortality statistics as presented on the CDC website https://tinyurl.com/CDCmortality accessed on May 2021. This table shows rate ratios compared to the group 5- to 17-year-olds (selected as the reference group because it has accounted for the largest cumulative number of COVID-19 cases compared to other age groups).

	0—4 years	5—17 years	18—29 years	30—39 years	40—49 years	50—64 years	65—74 years	75—84 years	85+ years
Cases[2]	<1x	Reference group	3x	2x	2x	2x	2x	2x	2x
Hospitalization[3]	2x	Reference group	7x	10x	15x	25x	35x	55x	80x
Death[4]	2x	Reference group	15x	45x	130x	400x	1100x	2800x	7900x

R snippets

A predictive model is a function that transforms the $n \times p$ data frame with p variables for n observations into a vector of n predictions. For further examples, below, we define a function that calculates odds of Covid related death based on statistics from the CDC website for different age groups[10].

```r
cdc_risk <- function(x, base_risk = 0.00003) {
  rratio <- rep(7900, nrow(x))
  rratio[which(x$Age < 84.5)] <- 2800
  rratio[which(x$Age < 74.5)] <- 1100
  rratio[which(x$Age < 64.5)] <- 400
  rratio[which(x$Age < 49.5)] <- 130
  rratio[which(x$Age < 39.5)] <- 45
  rratio[which(x$Age < 29.5)] <- 15
  rratio[which(x$Age < 17.5)] <- 1
  rratio[which(x$Age < 4.5)]  <- 2
  rratio * base_risk
}
steve <- data.frame(Age = 25, Diabetes = "Yes")
cdc_risk(steve)
## [1] 0.00045
```

Predictive models may have different structures. To work responsibly with a large number of models, a uniform standardized interface is needed. In this book, we use the abstraction implemented in the DALEX package[11].

The explain function from this package creates an *explainer*[12], i.e. a wrapper for the model that will allow you to work uniformly with objects of very different structures. The first argument is a model. It can be an object of any class. The second argument is a function that calculates the vector of predictions. DALEX package can often guess which function is needed for a specific model, but in this book, we show it explicitly in order to emphasize how the wrapper works. The type argument specifies the model type and the label specifies a unique name that appear in the plots.

```r
library("DALEX")
model_cdc <- DALEX::explain(cdc_risk,
              predict_function = function(m, x) m(x),
              type  = "classification",
              label = "CDC")
predict(model_cdc, steve)
## [1] 0.00045
```

Using the explain function may seem like an unnecessary complication at the moment, but on the following pages, we show how it simplifies the work.

The biggest advantage of such a constructed object (explainer) is its standardized structure, to some degree independent of the internal structure of the model.

[10] There was no risk for the reference group in Table 3. It is not relevant if we are only interested in the ranking of relative risks. But to make the predictions easier to interpret we use here the relative risk determined on Polish data, which is 0.003% for the reference group.

[11] Przemyslaw Biecek. DALEX: Explainers for Complex Predictive Models in R. *Journal of Machine Learning Research*, 19(84):1–5, 2018. URL https://jmlr.org/papers/v19/18-416.html

[12] Explainer is an object/adapter that wraps a model and creates a uniform structure and interface for operations.

I GOT YOU! MY SUPER CONTACTS AT NIH WILL LET US GET THE DATA FOR MODEL VALIDATION!

JUST A COUPLE OF PHONE CALLS AND VOILÀ.

PAŃSTWOWY ZAKŁAD HIGIENY
HI BIT! WE'LL FIND SOMETHING FOR YOU!

DATA
DOWNLOADING
I CAN SEE ON MY PHONE YOU'VE JUST SENT TWO DATABASES.
PLEASE KEEP IT TO YOURSELF. IT'S SEMI-OFFICIAL, OK?

I'VE GOT AN EPIDEMIOLOGICAL INTERVIEW OF 10,000 COVID-19 POSITIVE PATIENTS TESTED IN SPRING 2021 AND THE SECOND DATABASE OF 10,000 COVID-19 POSITIVE PATIENTS TESTED IN SUMMER 2021.
HAVE YOU? AWESOME!
DO YOU KNOW WHAT THE COLLECTION OF SUCH DATA LOOKS LIKE? IT IS QUITE A COMPLEX AND MULTI-STAGE PROCESS.
THIS IS STEVE. HE'S GOT A HEADACHE...
... I'VE GOT A COUGH, TOO.
PLEASE, GET COVID-19 TESTED.
OH..
THE TEST TURNS OUT TO BE POSITIVE. NO REASON TO BE HAPPY.
HELLO. THIS IS THE SANITARY INSTITUTE. AS STEVE IS COVID-19 POSITIVE, WE NEED TO ASK HIM A FEW QUESTIONS AND RECORD THE ANSWERS IN OUR DATABASE.
AT THE LAB.
COVID-19
COVID-19 TEST
POSITIVE
STEVE: MALE
AGE: 40
COEXISTING DISEASES: NONE
DATABASE

Exploratory Data Analysis (EDA)

To build a model, we need good data. In Machine Learning, the word *good* means a large amount of representative data. Unfortunately, collecting representative data is neither easy nor cheap and often requires designing and conducting a specific experiment.

The best possible scenario is that one can design and run a study to collect the necessary data. In less comfortable situations, we look for "natural experiments," i.e., data that have been collected for another purpose but that can be used to build a model. Here we use the data[13] collected through epidemiological interviews. The number of interviewed patients is large, so we treat this data as representative, although unfortunately, this data only involves symptomatic patients who are tested positive for SARS-COV-2. Asymptomatic cases are more likely to be young adults.

The data is divided into two sets: `covid_spring` and `covid_summer`. The first set was acquired in spring 2020 and will be used as training data, while the second dataset was acquired in the summer and will be used for validation. In machine learning, model validation is performed on a separate data set called validation data. This controls the risk of overfitting an elastic model to the training data. If we do not have a separate set, then it is generated using cross-validation, out-of-sample, out-of-time or similar data splitting techniques.

R snippets

The R software offers hundreds of specialized solutions for exploratory data analysis. Certainly, many valuable solutions can be found in the book „R for Data Science"[14], but there are much more. Below we show just three examples. Let's start with loading the data.

```
covid_spring <- read.table("covid_spring.csv", sep =";",
                           header = TRUE)
covid_summer <- read.table("covid_summer.csv", sep =";",
                           header = TRUE)
```

We use the package `ggplot2` to draw a simple histogram for Age, and `ggmosaic` to draw a mosaic plot for `Diabetes`. Note that the plots in the margins are graphically edited, so they look slightly different from the plots generated by these short instructions.

```
# See Figure 4
library("ggplot2")
ggplot(covid_spring) +
    geom_histogram(aes(Age, fill = Death))
# See Figure 5
library("ggmosaic")
ggplot(data = covid_spring) +
    geom_mosaic(aes(x=product(Diabetes), fill = Death))
```

[13] Please note that the attached data are not the real data collected for epidemiological purposes, but artificially generated data preserving the structure and relationships in the actual data.

[14] Hadley Wickham and Garrett Grolemund. *R for Data Science: Import, Tidy, Transform, Visualize, and Model Data.* O'Reilly Media, Inc., 2017

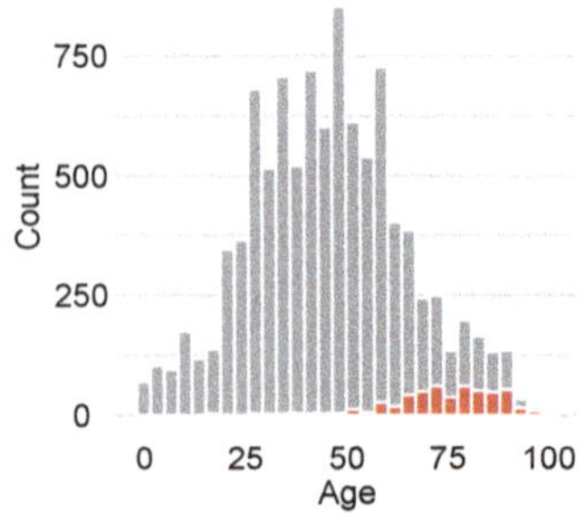

Figure 4: Histogram for the Age variable by survivor status.

A handy way to summarise tabular data in groups is the so-called „*Table 1*". This is a summary of the main characteristics of each variable broken down into groups defined by the variable of interest (here, binary information about Covid death). The name stems from the fact that this summary of the data is usually the first table to be shown in many medical and related scientific journals.

```
library("tableone")
CreateTableOne(vars = colnames(covid_spring)[1:10],
                        data = covid_spring,
                        strata = "Death")
#                                   Stratified by Death
#                                   No              Yes
#   n                               9487                 513
#   Gender = Male (%)               4554 (48.0)      271 (52.8)  0.037
#   Age (mean (SD))                 44.19 (18.32) 74.44 (13.2)  <0.001
#   CardiovascularDiseases = Yes (%)  839 ( 8.8)     273 (53.2)  <0.001
#   Diabetes = Yes (%)              260 ( 2.7)       78 (15.2)  <0.001
#   Neurological.Diseases = Yes (%)  127 ( 1.3)       57 (11.1)  <0.001
#   Kidney.Diseases = Yes (%)        111 ( 1.2)       62 (12.1)  <0.001
#   Cancer = Yes (%)                 158 ( 1.7)       68 (13.3)  <0.001
#   Hospitalization = Yes (%)       2344 (24.7)      481 (93.8)  <0.001
#   Fever = Yes (%)                 3314 (34.9)      335 (65.3)  <0.001
#   Cough = Yes (%)                 3062 (32.3)      253 (49.3)  <0.001
```

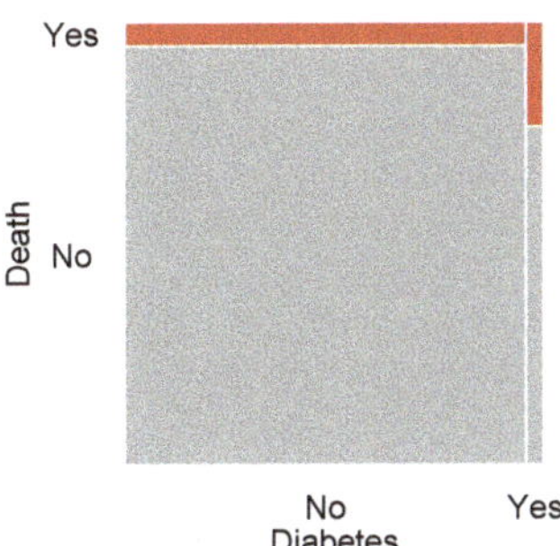

Figure 5: The mosaic plot shows that there are significantly fewer people with diabetes, but among them the mortality is higher.

One of the most important rules to remember when building a predictive model is: **Do not condition on future!**. I.e. do not use variables that are not defined at the time the prediction needs to be made. Note that in the discussed case variables Hospitalization, Fever or Cough are not good predictors because they are not known in advance before infection. So they are not useful in our case.

In the following lines, we remove invalid variables from both data sets.

```
selected_vars <- c("Gender", "Age", "Cardiovascular.Diseases",
    "Diabetes", "Neurological.Diseases", "Kidney.Diseases",
    "Cancer", "Death")
# use only selected variables
covid_spring <- covid_spring[,selected_vars]
covid_summer <- covid_summer[,selected_vars]
```

Data exploration and cleansing often consume most of the time spent on data analysis. Here we have only touched on exploration, but even this initial analysis helped to determine that Age is an important characteristic (we will confirm this later). From the list of variables we removed those that are unknown before the disease develops (like hospitalization status). We will build further models only on variables from the selected_vars vector.

Gender	Age	Cardiovascular Diseases	Diabetes	Neurological Diseases	Kidney Diseases	Cancer	Hospitalization	Fever	Cough	Weakness	Death
Male	29	No	No	No	No	No	No	No	No	No	No
Male	50	No	No	No	No	No	No	Yes	Yes	Yes	No
Male	39	No	No	No	No	No	No	No	No	No	No
Male	40	No	No	No	No	No	No	No	No	No	No
Male	53	No	No	No	No	No	No	Yes	Yes	Yes	No
Female	36	No	No	No	No	No	No	No	No	No	No
Female	56	No	No	No	No	No	No	Yes	Yes	No	No
Male	20	No	No	No	No	No	No	No	No	No	No
Female	59	No	No	No	No	No	No	No	No	No	No
Female	24	No	No	No	No	No	No	No	No	No	No
Male	43	No	No	No	No	No	No	No	No	No	No
Male	60	No	No	No	No	No	No	No	Yes	Yes	No
Female	12	No	No	No	No	No	No	No	No	No	No
Female	55	Yes	No	No	No	No	No	Yes	Yes	Yes	No
Female	53	No	No	No	No	No	No	Yes	Yes	Yes	No
Male	46	No	No	No	No	No	No	No	No	No	No
Female	81	Yes	No	No	Yes	No	Yes	Yes	Yes	No	
Female	59	No	No	No	No	No	Yes	No	Yes	No	
Female	51	No	No	No	No	No	Yes	No	No	No	

Sooo much data, sooo many interactions...
Coffee
Tea
COVID
19
60
5
55
50
10
45
15
40
20
35
25
30
30
20
10
No
Yes
No
Yes
No
No
No
No
No
No

Model Performance

Depending on the type of predictive problem and what we assume about the distribution of the outcome, various measures of model performance can be used. Here is a short summary; find a more detailed description in the EMA book.

For regression problems, when we predict a quantitative variable, especially when we assume Gaussian noise, commonly used performance measures are Mean Squared Error[15] and Rooted Mean Squared Error[16].

For binary classification problems, the outcome is commonly summarized with a 2×2 contingency table with possible results coded as True Positive, True Negative, False Positive, and False Negative. Positive means that the test suggests a pregnancy, while Negative means no pregnancy. True and False describe whether the test result is correct or not. Below is an example of such a table for a simple „morning sickness" test for the pregnancy.

[15] If $f : \mathcal{R}^p \to \mathcal{R}$ is a function that predicts the value of y_i using observation x_i, then
$$MSE = \tfrac{1}{n} \sum_i^n (f(x_i) - y_i)^2$$
[16] $RMSE = \sqrt{MSE}$

Morning sickness / pregnancy	Pregnant	Not pregnant	
Has sickness	**TP** = 39	**FP** = 150	PPV = Prec = 20.6%
Has not	**FN** = 61	**TN** = 850	NPV = 93.3%
	Sensitivity = Recall = 39%	Specificity = 85%	F1 = 33.8%

Table 1: Is morning sickness a good pregnancy test? This table is based on GetTheDiagnosis data http://getthediagnosis.org/diagnosis/Pregnancy.htm. For example, FN = 61 means that out of 100 pregnant women for 61 the test suggested otherwise. Exemplary measures of performance are shown in the last row and column.

Based on such a contingency table, the most commonly used measures of performance are Accuracy[17], Sensitivity[18], Specificity[19], Precision[20], Recall[21], F1 score[22], Positive Predicted Value[23] and Negative Predicted Value[24].

Note that in the covid-mortality-risk-assessment problem, we are not interested in the binary prediction survived/dead, but rather in the validity of the ranking of risk scores. For such types of problems, instead of a contingency table, one looks at Receiver Operating Characteristic (ROC) curve, and the commonly used measure of performance is the Area Under the ROC Curve (AUC). Figure 6 shows how this measure is constructed.

[17] $Acc = (TP + TN)/n$
[18] $Sens = TP/(TP + FN)$
[19] $Spec = TN/(TN + FP)$
[20] $Prec = TP/(TP + FP)$
[21] $Recall = TP/(TP + FN)$
[22] $F1 = 2\frac{Prec*Recall}{Prec+Recall}$
[23] $PPV = TP/(TP + FP)$
[24] $NPV = TN/(TN + FN)$

Figure 6: Panel A shows the distribution of scores obtained from the CDC model for the test data divided by the survival status. By taking different cutoffs, one can turn such numerical scores into binary decisions. For each such a split, the Sensitivity and 1-Specificity can be calculated and drawn on a plot.

Panel B shows 10 points corresponding to different splits. The ROC curve is the piecewise line connecting these points and the AUC is the area under this curve. The AUC takes values from 0 to 1, where 1 is the perfect ranking and a purely random ranking leads to the AUC of 0.5.

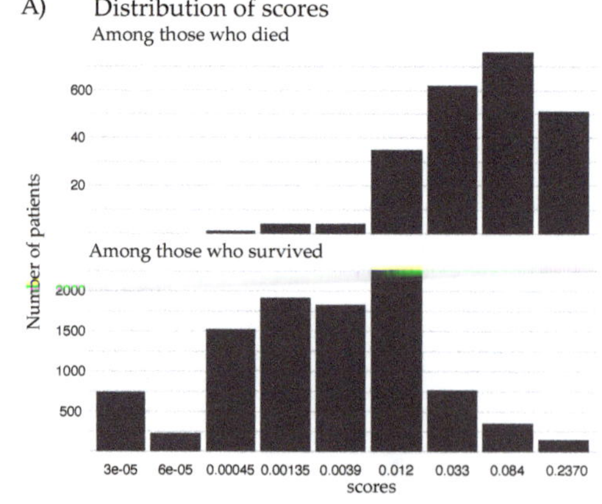

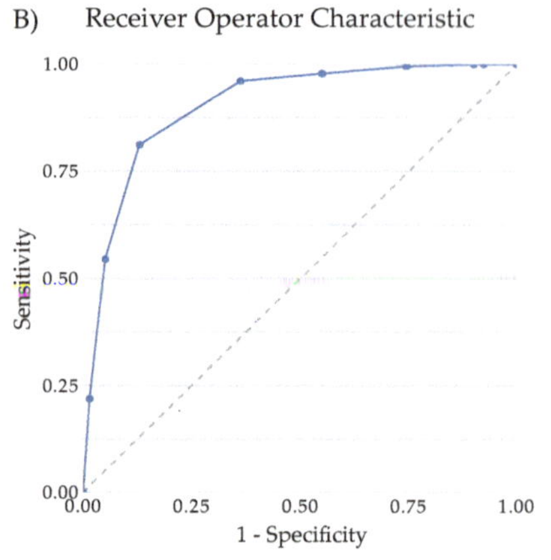

R snippets

There are many measures for evaluating predictive models, and they are implemented in various R packages (i.e. `ROCR`, `measures`, `mlr3measures`). For simplicity, in this example we show only model performance measures implemented in the `DALEX` package.

First, we need an explainer with specified validation data (here `covid_summer`) and the corresponding response variable.

```r
model_cdc <-  DALEX::explain(cdc_risk,
                  predict_function = function(m, x) m(x),
                  data  = covid_summer,
                  y     = covid_summer$Death == "Yes",
                  type  = "classification",
                  label = "CDC")
```

Model exploration starts with an assessment of how good is the model. The `DALEX::model_performance` function calculates a set of measures for a specified type of task, here classification.

```r
mp_cdc <- model_performance(model_cdc, cutoff = 0.1)
mp_cdc

# Measures for:  classification
# recall      : 0.2188841
# precision   : 0.2602041
# f1          : 0.2377622
# accuracy    : 0.9673
# auc         : 0.906654
#
# Residuals:
#       0%        10%        20%        30%        40%        50%
# -0.23700  -0.03300  -0.01200   -0.01200  -0.00390  -0.00390
#      60%        70%        80%        90%       100%
# -0.00135  -0.00135  -0.00045   -0.00006   0.99955
```

Note: The model is evaluated on the data given in the explainer. Use `DALEX::update_data()` to specify another dataset, e.g. training data `covid_spring`.

```r
model_cdc <-  update_data(model_cdc,
                  data  = covid_spring,
                  y     = covid_spring == "Yes")
```

Note: The explainer knows whether the model is trained for classification or regression task, so it automatically selects the right performance measures. This can be overridden if needed.

The S3 generic `plot` function draws a graphical summary of the model performance. With the `geom` argument, one can determine the type of chart.

```r
# ROC curve, see Figure 6
plot(mp_cdc, geom = "roc")
# LIFT curve, see Figure 7
plot(mp_cdc, geom = "lift")
```

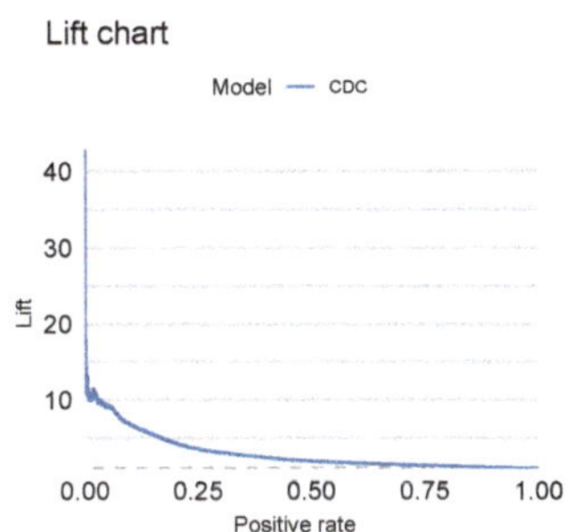

Figure 7: LIFT curve, one of the many graphical statistics used in summarizing the quality of scores, often used in credit risk scoring. The OX axis presents the fraction of assigned credits, and the OY axis presents the ratio of the Sensitivity of the tested model to the Sensitivity of the random model.

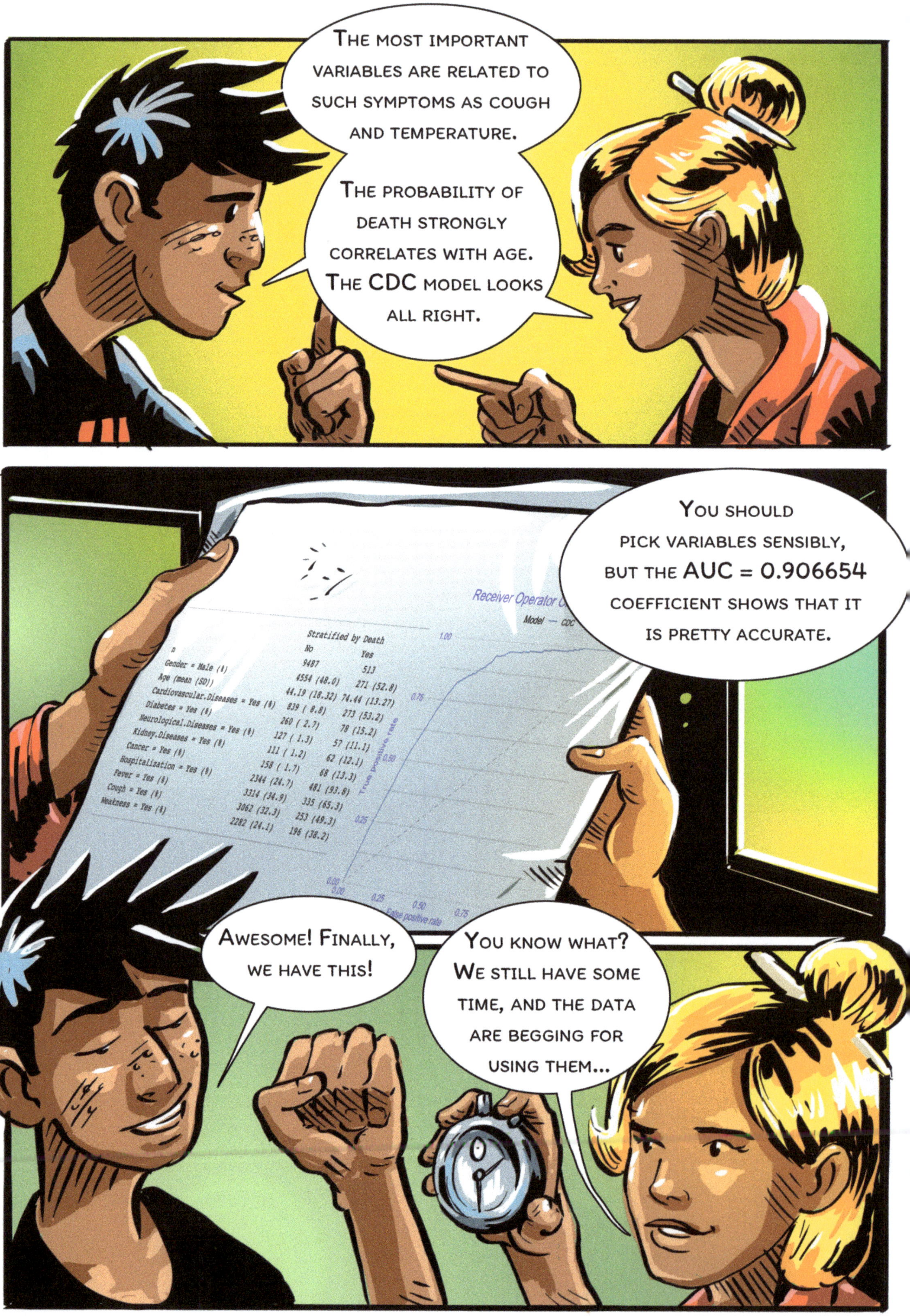

	Stratified by Death	
	No	Yes
n	9487	513
Gender = Male (%)	4554 (48.0)	271 (52.8)
Age (mean (SD))	44.19 (18.32)	74.44 (13.27)
Cardiovascular.Diseases = Yes (%)	839 (8.8)	273 (53.2)
Diabetes = Yes (%)	260 (2.7)	78 (15.2)
Neurological.Diseases = Yes (%)	127 (1.3)	57 (11.1)
Kidney.Diseases = Yes (%)	111 (1.2)	62 (12.1)
Cancer = Yes (%)	158 (1.7)	68 (13.3)
Hospitalization = Yes (%)	2344 (24.7)	481 (93.8)
Fever = Yes (%)	3314 (34.9)	335 (65.3)
Cough = Yes (%)	3062 (32.3)	253 (49.3)
Weakness = Yes (%)	2282 (24.1)	196 (38.2)

You're right. Let's go and get some fresh air. We can come up with something.
Well, I've already got an idea...

Have you ever heard of a predictive technique known as a decision tree?
Nope. Do you think it could be better than our CDC model?
We've got time and data. Any respectable researcher would jump at the opportunity to improve the model.

Besides, I find it fascinating how predictive trees grow downwards unlike the ones in nature.
So, the case is far from closed.

Grow a tree

There are hundreds of different methods for training machine learning models available to experienced data scientists. One of the oldest and most popular are tree-based algorithms, first introduced in the book *Classification And Regression Trees*[25] and commonly called CART. Here is the general deescription for this class of algorithms.

1. Start with a single node (root) with a full dataset.
2. For a current node, find a candidate split for the data in this node. To do this, consider every possible variable, and for each variable, consider every possible cutoff (for a continuous variable) or a subset of levels (for a categorical variable). Select the split that maximizes the measure of separation (see below).
3. Check a stopping criteria like the minimum gain in node purity or depth of a tree. If the stopping criteria are met, then (obviously) stop. Otherwise, partition the current node into two child nodes and go to step 2 for each child node separately.

There are two crucial choices here. The first one is the measure of separation. We illustrate it by considering splits of the Age variable for our dataset. For practical reasons, let's consider four groups.

[25] L. Breiman, J. H. Friedman, R. A. Olshen, and C. J. Stone. *Classification and Regression Trees.* Wadsworth and Brooks, Monterey, CA, 1984

Table 2: Number of patients that survived or died after the infection. Data divided into four separate age groups. Calculated for covid_spring data.

Age group / Status	$\leqslant 30$	31-50	51-70	>70	Total
Survived	2250	3716	2760	729	9487
Died	6	17	153	337	513
Total	2256	3733	2913	1066	10000

We consider three splits for cutoffs of 30, 50, and 70. For each split, we calculate the probability of death and survival in that group. We then calculate the purity[26] of each of the resulting nodes. In the example below, the Gini value is used, but entropy or statistical tests are also commonly used. The final split purity is defined as the weighted node purity considering the number of observations at each node. The smaller the value, the better. From the options below, we get the best purity for a cutoff of 70 years.

[26] For a categorical random variable with probability p_c for class c entropy is defined as
$$H = -\sum_c p_c \log_2 p_c,$$
while the Gini impurity
$$G = 1 - \sum_c p_c^2.$$
The Gini impurity for the root node in our example is 0.0973.

Table 3: Let us consider three possible splits of the variable Age, then step by step calculate the probabilities of each class, the purity of each node and the weighted purity of the split. The best split is for age 70, although for both the younger and older age groups the purity is worse than for the other splits. The weights defining the size of the nodes proved to be crucial in this example.

Possible split	30		50		70	
$node_i$	$\leqslant$	>	$\leqslant$	>	$\leqslant$	>
$p_{i,Died}$	0.0027	0.066	0.0038	0.123	0.0198	0.316
$p_{i,Surv}$	0.9973	0.934	0.9962	0.877	0.9802	0.684
$G_i = 1 - p_{i,Died}^2 - p_{i,Surv}^2$	0.0053	0.1228	0.00765	0.216	0.0388	0.4324
node weight w_i	0.2263	0.7737	0.6008	0.3992	0.8931	0.1070
$w_\leqslant G_\leqslant + w_> G_>$	0.0962		0.0908		0.0809	

The second key parameter for training a tree is the choice of the stopping criterion. Each split increases the purity of subsequent nodes, so the deeper the tree, the higher purity of leaves. Thus, large (deep) trees extract more relations from data, although some may be accidental (a phenomenon called over-fitting), which may result in poorer generalisation and worse results on new/validation data.

R snippets

There are many libraries in `R` for training decision trees. The following snippets are based on the `partykit`[27] library because it works for regression, classification and survival models and it also has good statistical properties and clear visualizations.

To train a tree, we use `ctree` function. The first argument is a formula describing which variable is the target and which are the explanatory variables[28]. The second argument indicates the training data. The `control` argument specifies additional parameters such as node splitting criteria, maximum tree depth or maximum node size.

```r
library("partykit")
tree <- ctree(Death ~., covid_spring,
              control = ctree_control(alpha = 0.0001))
# See Figure 8
plot(tree)
```

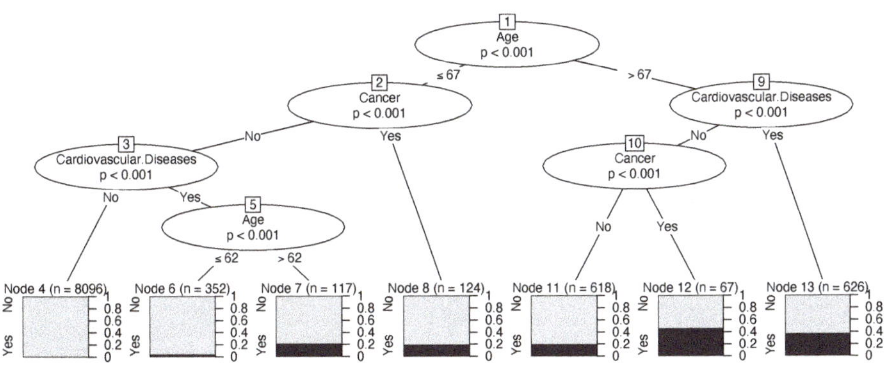
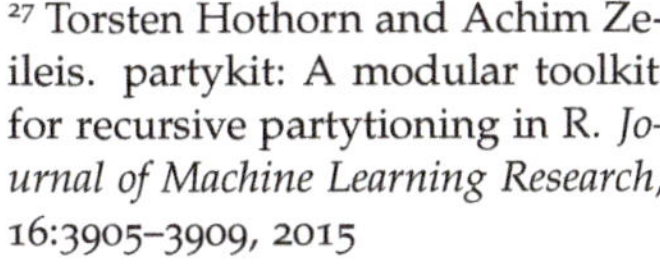

[27] Torsten Hothorn and Achim Zeileis. partykit: A modular toolkit for recursive partytioning in R. *Journal of Machine Learning Research*, 16:3905–3909, 2015

[28] In this package, statistical tests are used to evaluate separation for a split. In the example below, `alpha = 0.0001` means that nodes will be split as long as the p-value is below 0.0001 for the χ^2 test for independence.

Figure 8: The first split in the tree is for the Age variable. Patients are divided into younger than 67 (left) and older than 67 (right). In the same manner, one can read other splits. The criteria adopted resulted in a tree with seven leaves. The leaves include information about the number of patients who reached that leaf and the proportion of each class.

The `explain` function builds a uniform interface to query the model. Note that the `predict_function` is different than for CDC model, it is specific to `party` objects. The subsequent arguments indicate the test data for the explain count, model type and label.

```r
model_tree <- DALEX::explain(tree,
            predict_function = function(m, x)
                    predict(m, x, type = "prob")[,2],
            data = covid_summer,
            y = covid_summer$Death == "Yes",
            type = "classification", label = "Tree")
```

Once the explainer is prepared, we can check how good this model is. It looks like it is better than the CDC model both on the training and validation data.

```r
(mp_tree <- model_performance(model_tree, cutoff = 0.1))
# Measures for:  classification
# recall      : 0.8626609
# precision   : 0.1492205
# f1          : 0.2544304
# accuracy    : 0.8822
# auc         : 0.9136169
# See Figure 9
plot(mp_tree, mp_cdc, geom="roc")
```

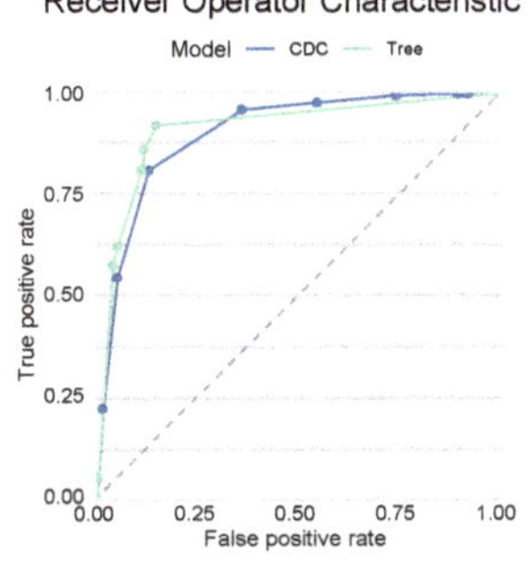

Figure 9: ROC curves for the CDC and tree model. The tree model has on average better predictions.

AND THIS IS THE TREE WE HAVE BUILT.
NOT BAD, THE MODEL USES BOTH THE INFO ABOUT AGE AND DISEASES. WE GET 7 RISK GROUPS.
PRINTING
Cardiovascular Diseases p < 0.001
Cancer p < 0.001
Age p < 0.001
Age p < 0.001
Cancer p < 0.001
Cardiovascular Diseases p < 0.001
THE PERFORMANCE OF THE DECISION TREE BASED ON NIH'S DATA IS EVEN BETTER.
Receiver Operator Characteristic
Model — CDC — Tree
True positive rate
False positive rate
THE AUC = 0.9136169 IS BETTER THAN THE ONE WITH THE CDC MODEL.
YOU SEE! WE'VE CRACKED IT. AND IT'S BEEN ONLY AN HOUR!
1H

Hang on. We have made a better model, perhaps we could make an even better one?
Leo Breiman. A distinguished statistician. (University of California) 1928-2005
Been recently reading about a random forest. A marvellous method for data analysis. Devised by Leo Breiman.
This technique makes it possible to combine hundreds of decision trees into one super model — a random forest.
Let's not focus on one tree when there's a whole forest ahead of us! As for me, the case is far from closed. Time for more analyses.

Plant a forest

Decision trees have many advantages, especially when it comes to interpretability and transparency. From a modelling perspective, deep trees have low bias but high variance (easily overfit to the data), while shallow trees have low variance but high bias (do not catch some relations). Can we improve both flexibility and stability?

In 2001, Leo Breiman proposed a new family of models, called random forests[29], which aggregate decisions from an ensemble of deep trees trained on bootstrap samples of the data. Bootstrap[30] is today a very widespread and powerful statistical procedure. It creates B copies of the data, called bootstrap samples, by sampling with replacement. One tree is trained on each copy of the data. During the prediction phase, the results from particular trees are aggregated. See Figure 10 for more details. Such a procedure improves model generalization by reducing the variance of individual trees.

Training a random forest model requires specification of hyperparameters such as B - the number of trees, m - the size of the subset of variables from which to select split candidates for a single node, maximum tree depth, minimum node size, etc. You will find more about the selection of hyperparameters in the next section, but fortunately the random forest algorithm is quite robust to the selection of hyperparameters. Thanks to all these advantages, random forest is a very popular and efficient technique for predictive modelling.

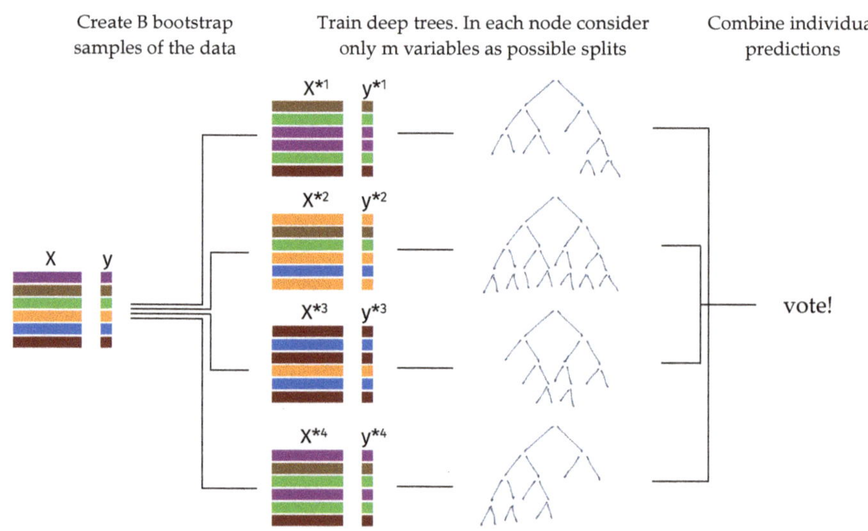

Figure 10: The key steps are: to generate a set of B bootstrap copies of the dataset by sampling rows with replacement. Deep trees are trained for each copy. To increase the variability between trees, the procedure for split selection is changed in a way that only a random subset of m variables is considered for a single node. During the prediction, the results of the individual trees are aggregated. Boostrap samples have out-of-bag (OOB) subsets, i.e. observations there were not selected during sampling on which the performance of the model can be evaluated. A detailed description of the random forest algorithm is available at
`https://tinyurl.com/RF2001`.

R snippets

The two most popular packages for training random forests in R are `randomForest`[31] and `ranger`[32]. Both are easy to use, efficient and well parameterized. But here we use `mlr3` toolkit for model training. It adds an additional level of abstraction, is a little more complex to use, but has additional features that will be used in the next section devoted to hyperparameters.

[29] Leo Breiman. Random forests. *Machine Learning*, 45(1):5–32, 2001a. ISSN 0885-6125

[30] The term bootstrap refers to the saying "pull oneself up by one's bootstraps" which relates to one of the tales of Baron Munchausen. It means to solve an impossible problem without outside help. In the original, the Baron pulled himself out of the swamp by his own hair. In the case of random forests, we have no new data, yet by creating bootstrap copies, we are able to control and reduce the variance of the predictive model.

[31] Andy Liaw and Matthew Wiener. Classification and Regression by randomForest. *R News*, 2(3):18–22, 2002

[32] Marvin N. Wright and Andreas Ziegler. ranger: A fast implementation of random forests for high dimensional data in C++ and R. *Journal of Statistical Software*, 77(1):1–17, 2017

Training a model with `mlr3`[33] is performed in three steps.

[33] Michel Lang, Martin Binder, Jakob Richter, Patrick Schratz, Florian Pfisterer, Stefan Coors, Quay Au, Giuseppe Casalicchio, Lars Kotthoff, and Bernd Bischl. mlr3: A modern object-oriented machine learning framework in R. *Journal of Open Source Software*, 2019. DOI: 10.21105/joss.01903

1. Define the prediction task, an object that remembers the training data and the target, i.e. the variable that should be predicted

```
library("mlr3")
(covid_task <- TaskClassif$new(id = "covid_spring",
        backend = covid_spring,
        target = "Death",  positive = "Yes"))
# <TaskClassif:covid_spring> (10000 x 8)
# * Target: Death
# * Properties: twoclass
# * Features (7):
#    - fct (6): Cancer, Cardiovascular.Diseases, Diabetes,
#      Gender, Kidney.Diseases, Neurological.Diseases
#    - int (1): Age
```

2. Select the family of models in which we want to look for a solution. There are a lot of algorithms to choose from, see the documentation. Set `"classif.ranger"` for the random forests models.

```
library("mlr3learners")
library("ranger")
covid_ranger <- lrn("classif.ranger", predict_type="prob",
                num.trees=25)
```

3. Train the model with the `train()` method. The `mlr3` package uses R6 classes, so this method modifies the object in place.

```
covid_ranger$train(covid_task)
```

A trained model can be turned into a `DALEX` explainer. Note that the `predict_function` is again slightly different. `DALEX` would guess this function based on the class of the model, but we point it out explicitly to make it easier to understand what is going on.

```
model_ranger <- explain(covid_ranger,
        predict_function = function(m,x)
            predict(m, x, predict_type = "prob")[,1],
        data = covid_summer,
        y = covid_summer$Death == "Yes",
        type = "classification", label = "Ranger")
```

We can now check how good this model is. As expected, a random forest model has better performance/AUC than a single tree.

```
(mp_ranger <- model_performance(model_ranger))
# Measures for:  classification
# recall      : 0.04291845
# precision   : 0.4347826
# f1          : 0.078125
# accuracy    : 0.9764
# auc         : 0.9425837


# See Figure 11
plot(mp_ranger, mp_tree, mp_cdc, geom= "roc")
```

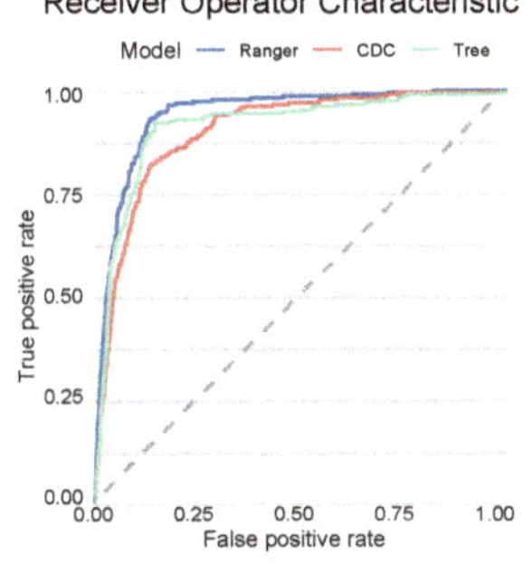

Figure 11: ROC curves for the CDC, tree and ranger model.

NOW WE'VE GOT A VERY COMPLEX MODEL. DIFFERENT TREES USE DIFFERENT VARIABLES AND IT'S EASY TO GET LOST IN THE PLETHORA OF OPTIONS. YOU GET THE RESULT IN A MAJORITY VOTE OF TREES.
YOU CAN'T DO IT ON A PIECE OF PAPER. YOU NEED A COMPUTER WITH SOME COMPUTING POWER TO CONSTRUCT A MODEL LIKE THIS.
HOW DO YOU LIKE OUR WALK IN A VIRTUAL FOREST?
IT'S GORGEOUS. LOOK HOW LOVELY IS THE COEFFICIENT WE GET.
Receiver Operator Characteristic
Model   Ranger   CDC   Tree
True positive rate
False positive rate
1.00
0.75
0.50
0.25
0.00
0.00   0.25   0.50   0.75   1.00
AUC = 0.9425837. EVEN BETTER THAN BEFORE.
WE'RE DONE IN LESS THAN AN HOUR!

Easy, no rush. To construct a random forest, we specified a few hyperparameters.
Perhaps we can create an even better model if we set the hyperparameters optimally?
Like automatic model optimization. I read about it on the net. You can try and test thousands of solutions and choose the best one.
No final solution yet. Hyperparameters are waiting for optimization!
But our computers are not fast enough for an analysis like this. We need a cluster.
I can fix that. I'll call one mate that's looking after Bambi.

Hyperparameter Optimisation

Machine Learning algorithms typically have many hyperparameters that specify a model training process. For some model families, like Support Vector Machines (SVM) or Gradient Boosting Machines (GBM), the selection of such hyperparameters has a strong impact on the performance of the final model. The process of finding good hyperparameters is commonly called *tuning*.

The general optimization scheme[34] is described in Figure 12. Different model families have different sets of hyperparameters. We don't always want to optimize all of them simultaneously, so the first step is to define the hyperparameter search space. Once it is specified, then tuning is based on a looped two steps: (1) select a set of hyperparameters and (2) evaluate how good this set of hyperparameters is. These steps are repeated until some stopping criterion is met, such as the maximum number of iterations, desired minimum model performance, or some increase in model performance.

[34] Each of the following steps can be implemented in many ways, so there is no single best way to tune models. We show an example framework for tabular data.

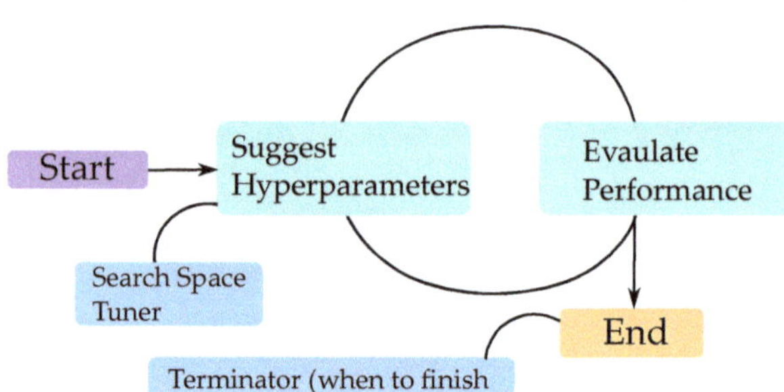

Figure 12: The hyperparameter optimization scheme implemented in the `mlr3tuning` package. Source: `https://mlr3book.mlr-org.com/tuning.html`

Let's focus more on the process of evaluating sets of hyperprameters. One of the key principles of machine learning is that the model should be verified on different data than that used for training. Even if we have separate data for training and final testing, we must not sneak a peek or use that test data when evaluating hyperparameters. We need to generate internal test data for the hyperparameter evaluation. This is often done using internal cross-validation. See an example on the next page.

R snippets

The example below uses the `mlr3` package. Other interesting solutions for hyperparameter optimization in R are `h2o` and `tidymodels`.

First, we need to specify the space of hyperparameters to search. Not all hyperparameters are worth optimizing. Let's focus on four for the random forest algorithm.

```
library("mlr3tuning")
library("paradox")
search_space = ps(
    num.trees = p_int(lower = 50, upper = 500),
    max.depth = p_int(lower = 1, upper = 10),
    minprop = p_dbl(lower = 0.01, upper = 0.1),
    splitrule = p_fct(levels = c("gini", "extratrees")))
)
```

For automatic hyperparameter search, it is necessary to specify: (1) a procedure to evaluate the performance of the proposed models (below it is the AUC determined by 5-fold cross-validation), (2) a search strategy for the parameter space (below it is a random search), (3) a stopping criterion (below it is the number of 10 evaluations[35]).

```
tuned_ranger = AutoTuner$new(
    learner     = covid_ranger,
    resampling = rsmp("cv", folds = 5),
    measure    = msr("classif.auc"),
    search_space = search_space,
    terminator = trm("evals", n_evals = 10),
    tuner      = tnr("random_search") )
```

Once the optimization parameters have been defined, we can turn on their optimization with the `train` method, just as with any other predictive model in `mlr3` framework[36].

```
tuned_ranger$train(covid_task)
tuned_ranger$tuning_result
#     num.trees max.depth     minprop splitrule
# 1:       264         9 0.06907318      gini
#     learner_param_vals  x_domain classif.auc
# 1:            <list[4]> <list[4]>   0.9272979
```

There is, of course, no guarantee that the tuner will find better hyperparameters than the default ones[37]. But in this example, the tuned model is better than all other models that we have considered so far. Let's see how much. We need a `DALEX` wrapper.

```
model_tuned <- explain(tuned_ranger,
    predict_function = function(m,x)
        m$predict_newdata(newdata = x)$prob[,1],
    data = covid_summer,
    y = covid_summer$Death == "Yes",
    type = "classification", label = "AutoTune")
```

We can calculate and compare the model performance/AUC on validation data and then compare ROC curves for various models.

```
(mp_tuned <- model_performance(model_tuned))
# Measures for:  classification
# recall     : 0.02575107
# precision  : 0.4
# f1         : 0.0483871
# accuracy   : 0.9764
# auc        : 0.9447171
# See Figure 13
plot(mp_tuned, mp_ranger, mp_tree, mp_cdc, geom = "roc")
```

Note on reproducibility: Take into account that the training is based on randomization, so you may get slightly different results on different computers or with different versions of packages. Even if you execute the same snippet twice, you may get slightly different results. Nevertheless, the general conclusions should be the same.

[35] Of course, Bit having a High Performance Cluster (HPC) can check hundreds of thousands of hyperparameter configurations as the whole process is easily parallelized. However, in this example we have focused on reproducibility, so we present results for 10 configurations, making it easy for any reader to reproduce these results. Also, for this dataset, the default random forest hyperparameters give very good results, so we wouldn't gain much with long tuning anyway.

[36] Note that the AUC 0.9272979 presented below is not calculated on the `covid_summer`, but it is an internal evaluation of hyperparameters with the 5-fold CV procedure. AUC on the `covid_summer` is presented at the bottom of this page.

[37] Moreover, some algorithms, like random forests, are not very tunable. Still, we had to try!

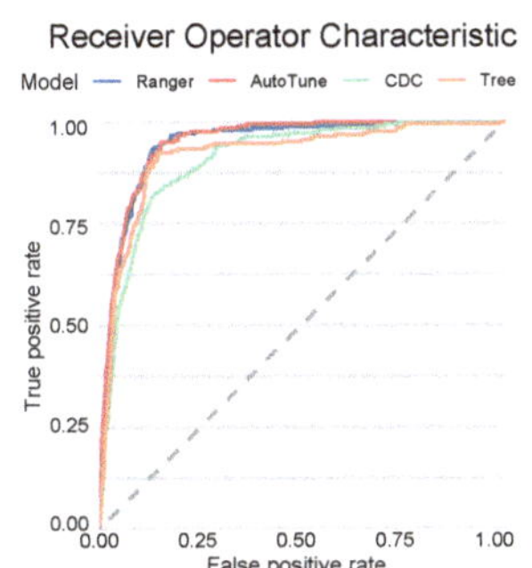

Figure 13: ROC curves for the CDC, tree, ranger model and auto tune ranger model.

CHECK THIS OUT. THAT'S "BAMBI" COMPUTATIONAL CLUSTER, WHICH HAS BEEN WORKING FOR THE PAST HOUR UTILISING THOUSANDS OF PROCESSES. BUT, IT'S LIKE SPENDING THOUSANDS OF HOURS DOING CALCULATIONS.

Receiver Operator Characteristic
Model — AutoTune — Ranger — CDC — Tree
True positive rate
1.00
0.75
0.50
0.25
0.00
False positive rate
0.00 0.25 0.50 0.75 1.00
AND AGAIN, WE'VE GOT A MORE EFFICIENT MODEL THAN BEFORE... AUC = 0.9447171. I WONDER IF IT CAN STILL GET BETTER.
HOLD ON. WAIT. WE'VE GOT WHAT WE WANTED. WE'VE GOT LITTLE TIME NOW. LET'S GO AND GET SOME COFFEE AND TALK ABOUT IT.

WE HAVE FOUR ITERATIONS. AN EXCELLENT MODEL, EVEN A FEW MODELS. WE'VE GOT LITTLE TIME, THAT'S A FACT.
PLEEEEEASE, SAY IT!
ALL RIGHT. WE'VE CRACKED IT!

BUT... WE CAN'T RESPONSIBLY RECOMMEND THIS MODEL IF WE DON'T KNOW HOW IT WORKS.
IT WORKS. WHAT ELSE DO YOU NEED?
IT'S ABOUT OUR AGENTS' SAFETY. WE NEED TO TEST THIS MODEL THOROUGHLY.
EXPLAIN...
EXPLAIN...
EXPLAIN...
OH, HI DALEX!
HAVE YOU BEEN OUT TO FRESHEN UP YOUR CIRCUITS AFTER BIT'S LAST PROGRAMMING? I'LL BE HAPPY TO EXPLAIN EVERYTHING BECAUSE I HAVE AN IDEA HOW YOU COULD HELP US.
f(x)
AUC
RMSE
WE NEED TO DO A FULL ANALYSIS OF THE MODEL. WE CAN USE THE PYRAMID OF MODEL EXPLORATION. WE NEED TO CHECK HOW IMPORTANT THE INDIVIDUAL VARIABLES IN THE MODEL ARE AND YOU CAN REALLY BE OF GREAT HELP.

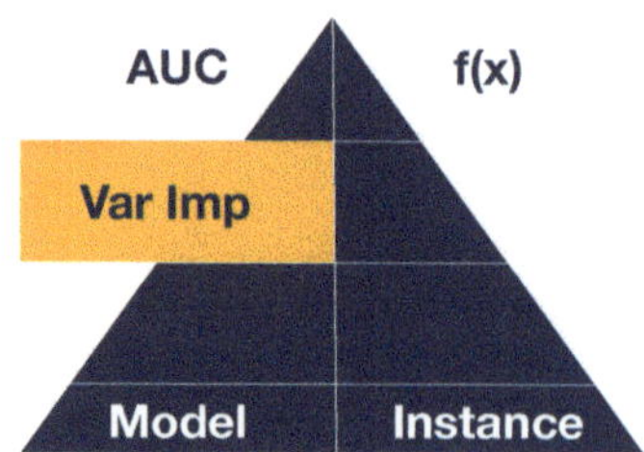

The XAI pyramid describes relations between explanatory model analysis techniques. The deeper, the more detailed view into the model.

[38] The permutational variable importance is described in detail in Chapter 16 of Explanatory Model Analysis https://ema.drwhy.ai/featureImportance.html

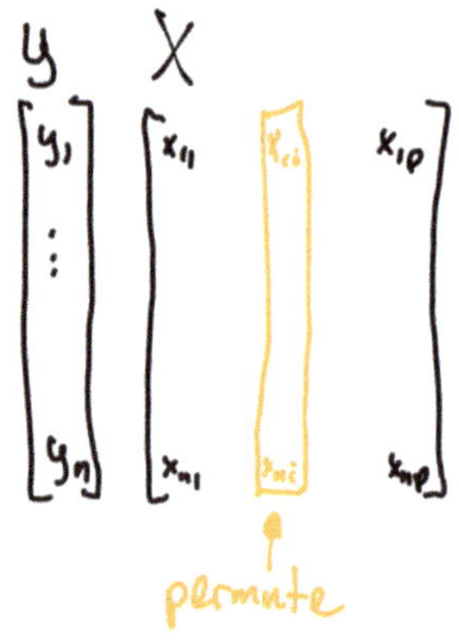

Figure 14: Permutation of variables preserves the marginal distribution while breaking the dependence of that variable on the target.

Variable-importance

When we examine a high-dimensional model, one of the first questions that come up are: *which variables are important? which features or groups of features significantly affect the model's performance?*

Some models have built-in methods for the assessment of variable importance. For example, for linear models, one can use standardized model coefficients or p-values. For the random forest, one can use out-of-bag classification error. For tree boosting models, one can use information gain statistics. Yet, the problem with such model-specific techniques is that they cannot be compared between models of different structures. For this and a few other reasons, it is convenient to use model agnostic techniques, such as permutational importance of variables[38].

The procedure is based on perturbations of a selected variable or group of variables. The intuition is that if a variable is important in a model, then after its random perturbation the model predictions should be less accurate.

The permutation-based variable-importance of a variable i is the difference (or ratio) between the model performance for the original data and the model performance calculated on data with the permuted variable i. More formally

$$VI(i) = L(f, X^{perm(i)}, y) - L(f, X, y),$$

where $L(f, X, y)$ is the value of loss function or performance measure for the data X, true labels y and model f, while $X^{perm(i)}$ is dataset x with i-th variable permuted.

Note that the importance of the variables defined in such a way can be determined without re-training of the model.

Which performance measure should you choose? It's up to you. In the DALEX library, by default, RMSE is used for regression and 1-AUC for classification problems. But you can change the loss function by specifying the loss_function argument.

R snippets

We use the model_parts function from the DALEX package to calculate the importance of variables. The only required argument is the model to be analyzed. With additional arguments, one can also specify how the importance of variables is to be calculated, whether as a difference, ratio or without normalization. The last line _baseline_ of the following listing corresponds to the difference in the loss function of a model calculated on data in which all variables have been permuted.

```
mpart_ranger <- model_parts(model_ranger, type="difference")
mpart_ranger
#                      variable mean_dropout_loss  label
# 1                 _full_model_      0.0000000000 Ranger
# 2    Neurological.Diseases      0.0006254491 Ranger
```

```
# 3                    Gender    0.0030246808 Ranger
# 4           Kidney.Diseases    0.0048972639 Ranger
# 5                    Cancer    0.0061278070 Ranger
# 6                  Diabetes    0.0076210243 Ranger
# 7   Cardiovascular.Diseases    0.0207565006 Ranger
# 8                       Age    0.1580579207 Ranger
# 9                _baseline_    0.4203818555 Ranger
```

This technique is handy when we want to compare the importance of variables in different models. Let's see what it looks like in our example. The generic `plot` function works for any number of models given as consecutive arguments.

```
mpart_cdc    <- model_parts(model_cdc)
mpart_tree   <- model_parts(model_tree)
mpart_ranger <- model_parts(model_ranger)
mpart_tuned  <- model_parts(model_tuned)
# See Figure 15
plot(mpart_cdc, mpart_tree, mpart_ranger, mpart_tuned,
              show_boxplots = FALSE)
```

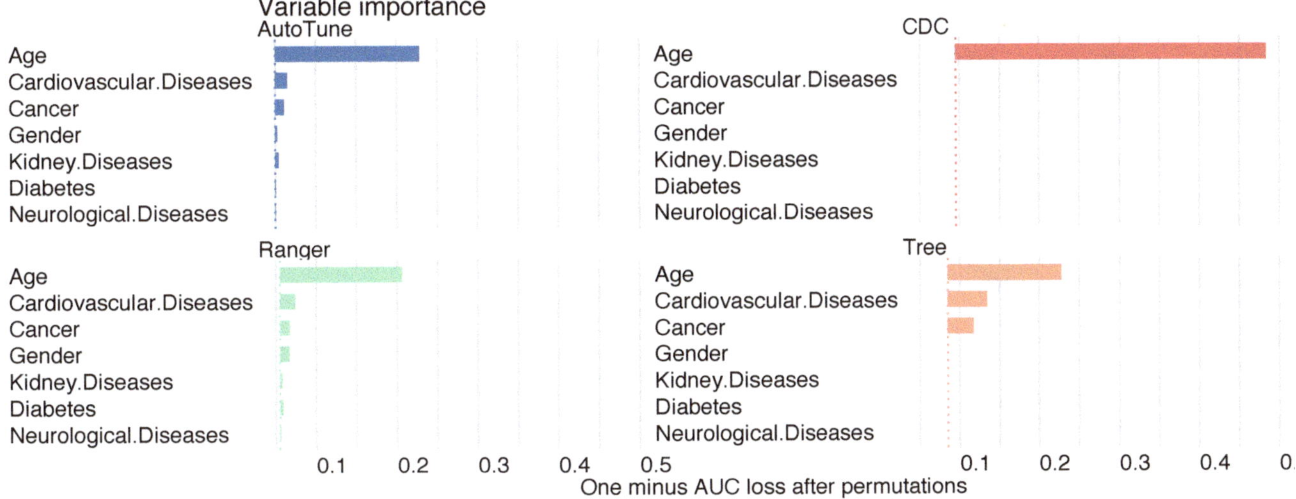

Figure 15: The importance of variables can be compared between various models, and it is usually a source of valuable information. In this plot, each bar starts at 1-AUC for the model on the original data and ends at 1-average AUC calculated on the data with the indicated variable permuted.

For the CDC model, the only important variable is Age. For the tree model, the three important variables are Age, Cancer, and Cardiovascular diseases, an observation consistent with Figure 8. For the ranger model and the model after tuning of hyperparameters, more variables are taken into account. However, Age is indisputably the most important variable in all models.

Looking for more?

The same perturbation technique can be used to analyze the importance of groups of variables. Just use the `variable_groups` argument. Grouping variables can be particularly useful if the number of variables is large and groups of variables describe some common aspects. In our case we could group all diseases together.

For highly correlated variables, an interesting model exploration technique is `triplot`, summarising correlations structure via a dendrogram and also show the importance of groups of correlated variables. Still, variable importance analysis when variables are correlated must be performed with care.

HERE ARE THE RESULTS FROM DALEX.
THE IMPORTANCE OF VARIABLES IN INDIVIDUAL MODELS IS SIMILAR. AGE IS NUMBER ONE BUT...
EXPLAIN! EXPLAIN! EXPLAIN! EXPLAIN! EXPLAIN! EXPLAIN!
HOLD ON. AGE SEEMS TO BE THE MOST IMPORTANT FACTOR IN THE ANALYSIS, BUT DIFFERENT MODELS EXTRACT INFORMATION FROM DIFFERENT VARIABLES. THE TWO MOST FREQUENT VARIABLES ARE HYPER-TENSION AND THE INFORMATION ABOUT POTENTIAL CANCER.
AT LAST. ALL CLEAR AND OBVIOUS
LET'S SEND IT. WE'VE ALMOST RUN OUT OF TIME.
LOOK. CLEAR AS DAY.
Variable importance
AutoTune
Age
Cardiovascular.Diseases
Cancer
Gender
Kidney.Diseases
Diabetes
Neurological.Diseases
Death
CDC
Age
Cardiovascular.Diseases
Cancer
Gender
Kidney.Diseases
Diabetes
Neurological.Diseases
Death
Ranger
Age
Cardiovascular.Diseases
Cancer
Gender
Kidney.Diseases
Diabetes
Neurological.Diseases
Death
Tree
Age
Cardiovascular.Diseases
Cancer
Gender
Kidney.Diseases
Diabetes
Neurological.Diseases
Death
0.0   0.1   0.2   0.3   0.4   0.5
One minus AUC loss after permutations

EASY! HASTE SPOILS EVERYTHING.
WE STILL HAVE SOME TIME. WHY NOT
TEST OTHER METHODS FROM THE PYRAMID OF MODEL
EXPLORATION? WE KNOW AGE MATTERS BUT HOW
DOES IT TRANSLATE INTO A RISK OF DEATH?
WE MUST USE OTHER TECHNIQUES, LIKE PARTIAL
DEPENDENCE, TO CHECK THE CORRELATION
BETWEEN THE AGE AND
MODEL RESULTS.
TRUE!
TRUE!
TRUE!

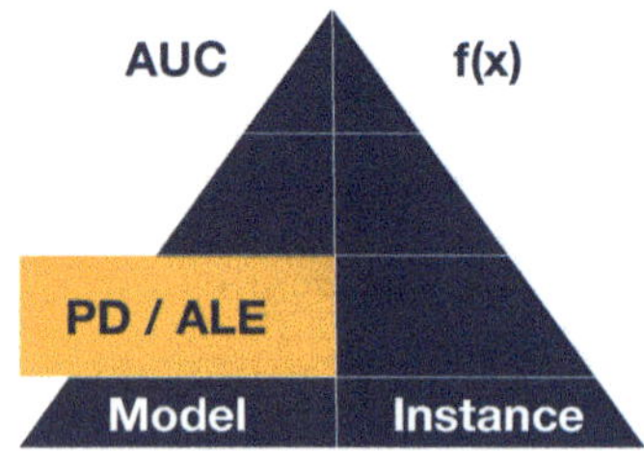

Both methods are described in detail in Chapter 17 of the Explanatory Model Analysis https://ema.drwhy.ai/partialDependenceProfiles.html

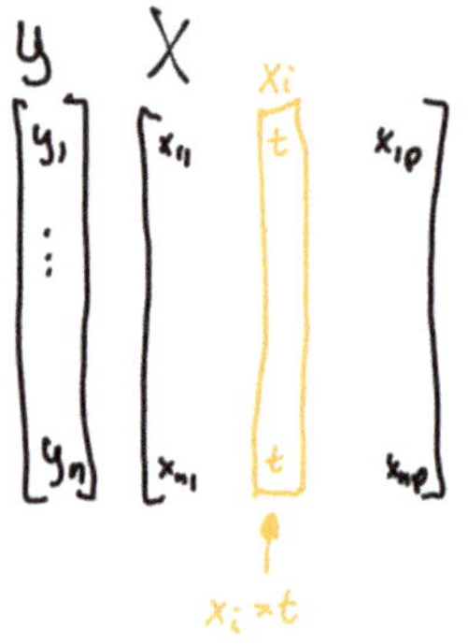

Figure 16: In the data set, the variable i is replaced by the value t, then an average model response is calculated.

Partial Dependence and Accumulated Local Effects

Once we know which variables are important, it is usually interesting to determine the relationship between a particular variable and the model prediction. Popular techniques for this type of Explanatory Model Analysis are Partial Dependence (PD) and Accumulated Local Effects (ALE).

PD profiles were initially proposed in 2001 for gradient boosting models but can be used in a model agnostic fashion. This method is based on analysis of average model response after replacing variable i with the value of t.

More formally, Partial Dependence profile for variable i is a function of t defined as

$$PD(i, t) = E\left[f(x_1, ..., x_{i-1}, t, x_{i+1}, ..., x_p)\right],$$

where the expected value is calculated over the data distribution. The straightforward estimator is

$$\widehat{PD}(i, t) = \frac{1}{n} \sum_{j=1}^{n} f(x_1^j, ..., x_{i-1}^j, t, x_{i+1}^j, ..., x_p^j).$$

Replacing i-th variable by value t can lead to very strange observations, especially when i-th variable is correlated with other variables and we ignore the correlation structure. One solution to this are Accumulated Local Effects profiles, which average over the conditional distribution.

Analysis of the Partial Dependence profile for each variable carries a lot of useful information. However, keep in mind that in complex models, you should expect complex interactions. Thus, one global profile for a variable may be an oversimplification. An extension of PD profiles is to calculate them in subgroups defined by some other variables or based on segments of observations found from model responses. You will find some examples below.

R snippets

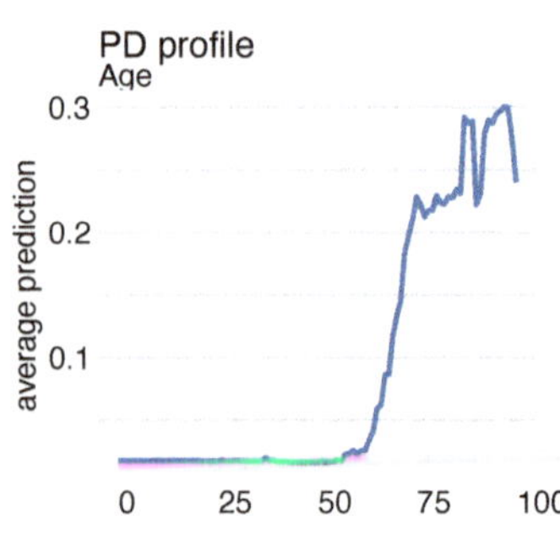

Figure 17: Partial dependence profile for Age variable.

We use the `model_profile` function from the **DALEX** package to calculate the variable profile. The only required argument is the model to be analyzed. It is a good idea to specify names of variables for profile estimation as a second argument; otherwise, profiles are calculated for all variables, which can take some time. One can also specify the exact grid of values for calculations of profiles.

The average is calculated for the distribution specified in the data argument in the explainer. Here we calculate the PD profiles for the Age variable for `covid_summer` data.

```r
mp_ranger <- model_profile(model_ranger, "Age")
# See Figure 17
plot(mp_ranger)
```

Since we have four models it is worth comparing how they differ in terms of the model's response to the Age variable.

```
mp_cdc     <- model_profile(model_cdc, "Age")
mp_tree    <- model_profile(model_tree, "Age")
mp_tuned   <- model_profile(model_tuned, "Age")
# See Figure 20
plot(model_cdc, model_tree, mp_ranger, model_tuned)
```

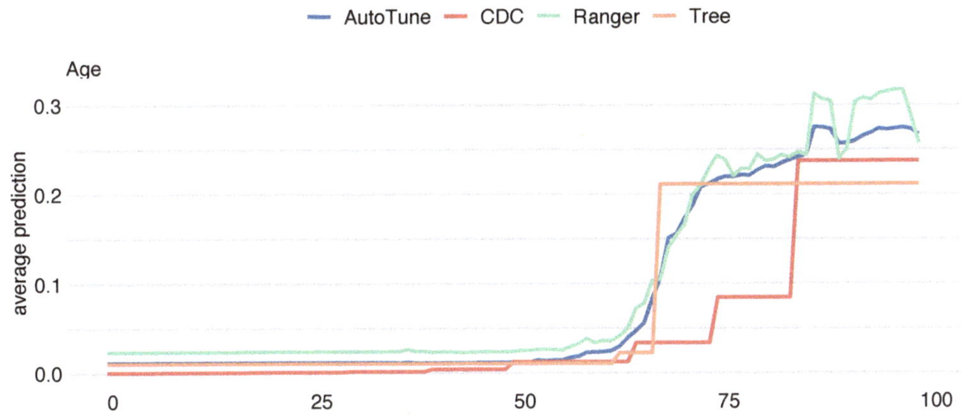

Figure 18: Each colour indicates a different model. The CDC model has a shifted sharp increase in risk of death. Models based on covid_spring data are more likely to place the dramatic increase in the risk around age 65. The tree model is too shallow to capture the ever-increasing risk in the oldest group. Despite this, the models are quite consistent about the general shape of the relationship.

Grouped Partial Dependence profiles

By default, the average is calculated for all observations. But with the argument `groups` one can specify a grouping variable. PD profiles are calculated independently for each level of this variable.

```
mgroup_ranger <- model_profile(model_ranger, "Age",
                     groups = "Diabetes")
# See Figure 19
plot(mgroup_ranger)
```

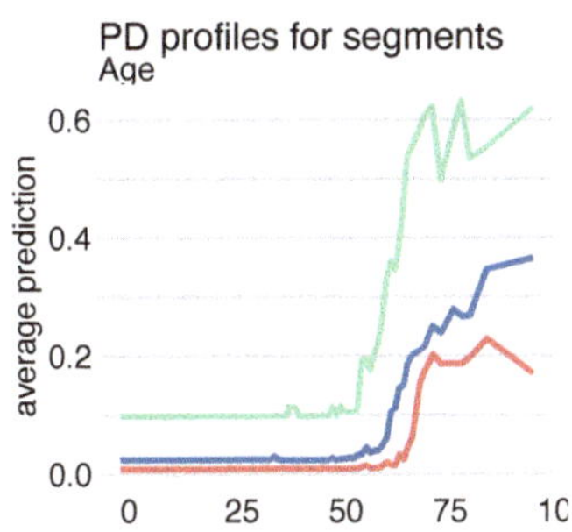

Figure 19: Partial Dependence for Age in groups defined by Diabetes variable.

Clustered Partial Dependence profiles

If the model is additive, then individual profiles (see the next Section related to *Ceteris Paribus* profiles) are parallel. But if the model has interactions, individual profiles may have different shapes for different values of variables in each interaction. To see if there are such interactions we can cluster the individual profiles.

If we specify the argument `k`, then the function `model_profile` performs a hierarchical clustering of the profiles, determines the group of k most different profiles and then calculates the Partial Dependence for each of these groups separately.

```
mclust_ranger <- model_profile(model_ranger, "Age",
                     k = 3, center = TRUE)
# See Figure 20
plot(mclust_ranger)
```


Figure 20: Partial Dependence for three segments.

LOOK AT THE EFFECT...
...OF THE VARIABLE AGE IN EACH MODEL.
Partial Dependence profile
Created for the AutoTune, CDC, Tree, Ranger model
AutoTune   CDC   Ranger   Tree
25   50   75   100
I'M LOOKING BUT WHAT'S IN IT FOR US?
FOR YOUNG AGENTS, ALL MODELS SUGGEST SIMILARLY LOW RISK.
65-80
≤30
BUT, THE TREE MODELS ASSIGN A HIGHER RISK OF DEATH FOR THOSE AGED 65-80 THAN THE CDC MODEL.
HA! THOSE ARE MINOR DIFFERENCES. ALL THE MODELS LOOK REASONABLE. DON'T SAY THEY DON'T! IN FACT, WE CAN SEND THEM TO MR. MI2. MISSION ACCOMPLISHED.

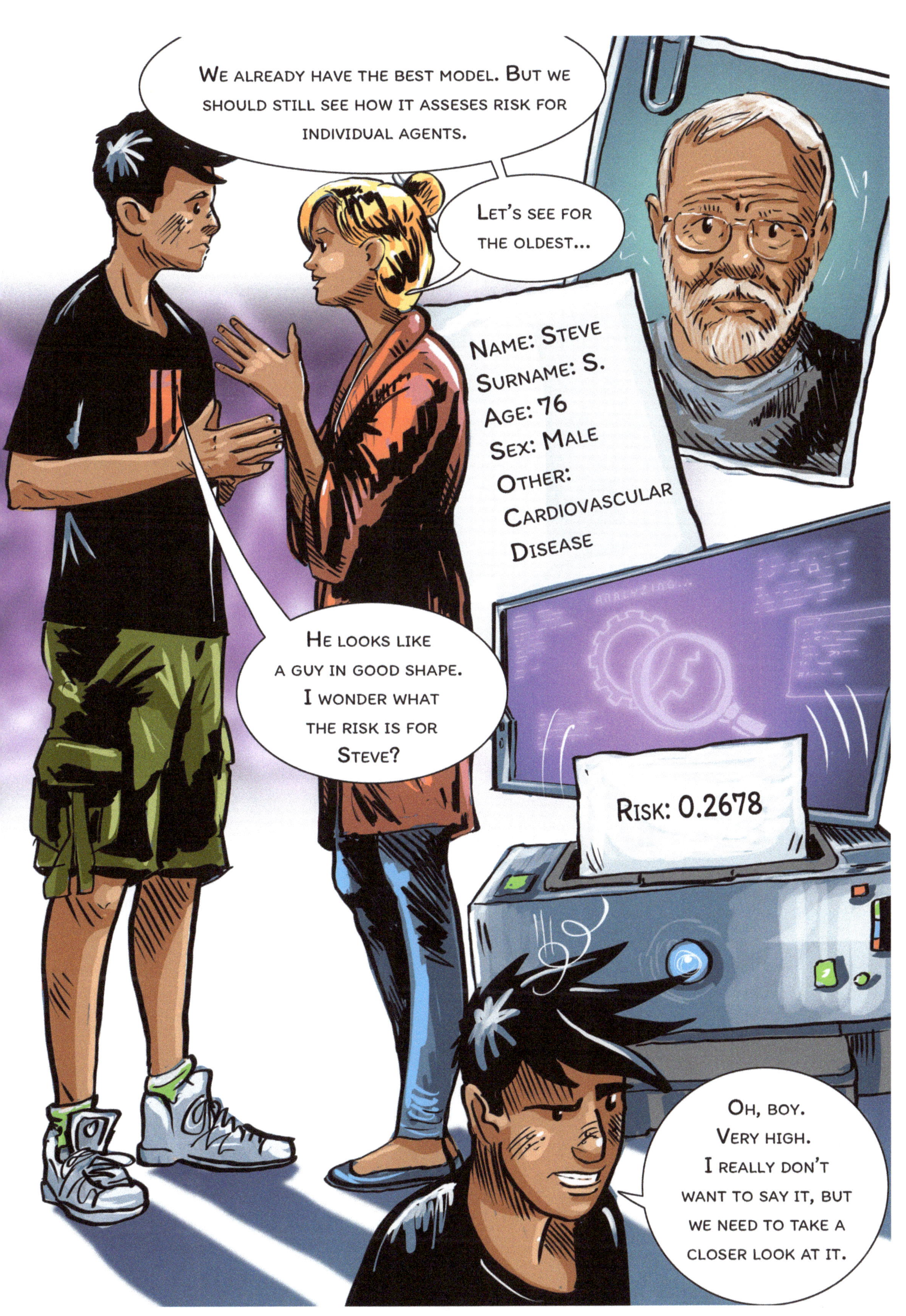

WE ALREADY HAVE THE BEST MODEL. BUT WE SHOULD STILL SEE HOW IT ASSESES RISK FOR INDIVIDUAL AGENTS.
LET'S SEE FOR THE OLDEST...
NAME: STEVE
SURNAME: S.
AGE: 76
SEX: MALE
OTHER: CARDIOVASCULAR DISEASE
HE LOOKS LIKE A GUY IN GOOD SHAPE. I WONDER WHAT THE RISK IS FOR STEVE?
RISK: 0.2678
OH, BOY. VERY HIGH. I REALLY DON'T WANT TO SAY IT, BUT WE NEED TO TAKE A CLOSER LOOK AT IT.

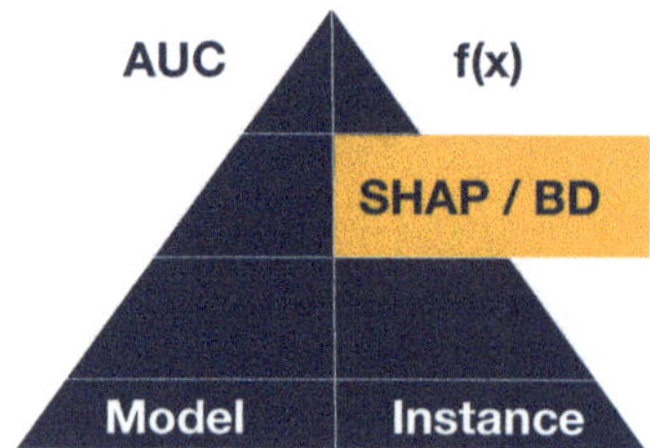

Instance level exploration

From the model developer perspective, we are often interested in the global behaviour of a model, i.e. whether it has high performance or how it changes on average as s function of some feature. But the user perspective is different. In most cases, a user is interested in an individual prediction related to him or her. Often we hear about the „right to explanation", which means that for a model prediction, we should be able to find out which variables significantly influenced the model prediction. Especially for high-stake decisions, we should enrich model predictions with as much information as possible to support informed and responsible predictions.

Shapley values and the Break-down plots

For tabular data, one of the most commonly used techniques for local variable attribution is Shapley values. The key idea behind this method is to analyze the sequence of conditional expected values. This way, we can trace how the conditional mean moves from the average model response to the model prediction for observation of interest x^*. Let's consider a sequence of expected values.

$$\mu = E\left[f(X)\right],$$
$$\mu_{x_1} = E\left[f(X)|X_1 = x_1^*\right],$$
$$\mu_{x_1,x_2} = E\left[f(X)|X_1 = x_1^*, X_2 = x_2^*\right],$$
$$\ldots$$
$$\mu_{x_1,x_2,\ldots,x_p} = E\left[f(X)|X_1 = x_1^*, X_2 = x_2^*, \ldots, X_p = x_p^*\right] = f(x^*).$$

By looking at consecutive differences $\mu_{x_1} - \mu$, $\mu_{x_1,x_2} - \mu_{x_1}$ and so on, one can calculate the added effects of individual variables, see an example in Figure 21. It sounds like a straightforward solution; however, there are two issues with this approach.

One is that it is not easy to estimate the conditional expected value. In most implementations, it is assumed that features are independent, and then we can estimate μ_K as an average model response with variables in the set K replaced by corresponding values from observation x^*. So the crude estimate would be

$$\widehat{\mu}_K = \frac{1}{n}\sum_{i=1}^{n} f(x_1^o, x_2^o, \ldots, x_p^o), \quad \text{where} \quad \begin{cases} x_j^o = x_j^*, \text{ if } j \in K \\ x_j^o = x_j^i, \text{ if } j \notin K. \end{cases}$$

The second issue is that these effects may depend on the order of conditioning. How to solve this problem? The Shapley values method calculates attributions as an average of all (or at least a large number of random) orderings, while the Break-down method uses a single ordering determined with a greedy heuristic that prefers variables with the largest attribution at the beginning.

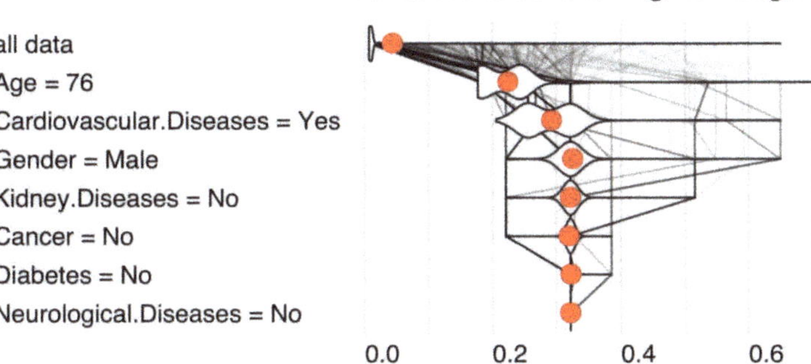

Figure 21: The following rows show the conditional distributions (vioplots) and the conditional expected value (red dot). The grey lines between the rows show how the predictions for each observation change after replacing the next variable with the value from observation x^*. Analyzing such a sequence of conditionings, we can read which variables significantly explain the differences between the mean model response (the first row) and the observed model response (the last row).

R snippets

Let's define an observation for which we will examine the model more closely. Let it be a 76-year-old man with hypertension. We show a local model analysis using `model_ranger` as an example.

```
Steve <- data.frame(Gender = factor("Male", c("Female", "Male")),
   Age                      = 76,
   Cardiovascular.Diseases = factor("Yes", c("No", "Yes")),
   Diabetes                 = factor("No", c("No", "Yes")),
   Neurological.Diseases    = factor("No", c("No", "Yes")),
   Kidney.Diseases          = factor("No", c("No", "Yes")),
   Cancer                   = factor("No", c("No", "Yes")))
predict(model_ranger, Steve)
# 0.322
```

The `predict_parts` function for a specified model and a specified observation calculates local variable attributions. The optional argument `order` forces use of a specified sequence of variables. If not specified, then a greedy heuristic is used to start conditioning with the most relevant variables. The results are presented in Figure 22.

```
(bd_ranger <- predict_parts(model_ranger, Steve))
#                                              contribution
# Ranger: intercept                                0.043
# Ranger: Age = 76                                 0.181
# Ranger: Cardiovascular.Diseases = Yes            0.069
# Ranger: Gender = Male                            0.033
# Ranger: Kidney.Diseases = No                    -0.004
# Ranger: Cancer = No                             -0.002
# Ranger: Diabetes = No                            0.003
# Ranger: Neurological.Diseases = No               0.000
# Ranger: prediction                               0.322
plot(bd_ranger)
```

The alternative is to average over all (or at least many random) orderings of variables. This is how the Shapley values are calculated. The `show_boxplots` argument highlights the stability of the estimated attributions between different orderings. See Figure 22.

```
shap_ranger <- predict_parts(model_ranger, Steve, type = "shap")
plot(shap_ranger, show_boxplots = TRUE)
```

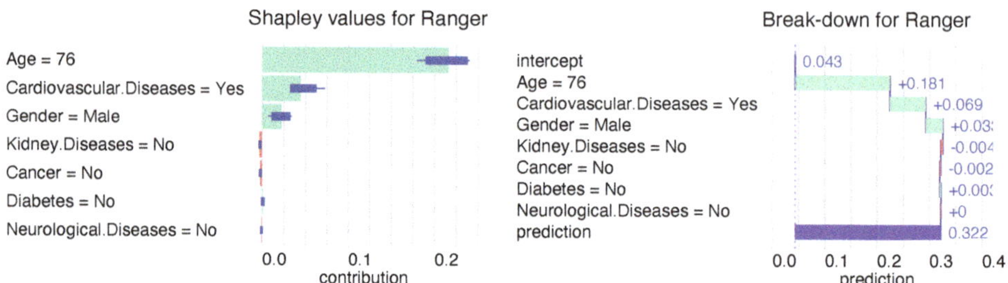

Figure 22: Shapley values (left) and Break-down (right) illustrate the contributions of each variable to the final model response. Both attribution techniques ensure that the sum of the individual attributions adds up to the final model prediction.

The Shapley values are additive. For models with interactions, it is often too much of simplification. Other possible values of the `type` argument are `shap`, `break_down`, `break_down_interactions`[39] or `oscillations`.

[39] This option can identify pairwise interactions, see Chapter 7 in `https://ema.drwhy.ai/iBreakDown.html`.

Note that by default, functions such as `model_parts`, `predict_parts`, `model_profiles` do not calculate statistics on the entire data set (this may be time-consuming), but on `n_samples` of random cases, and the entire procedure is repeated `B` times to estimate the error bars.

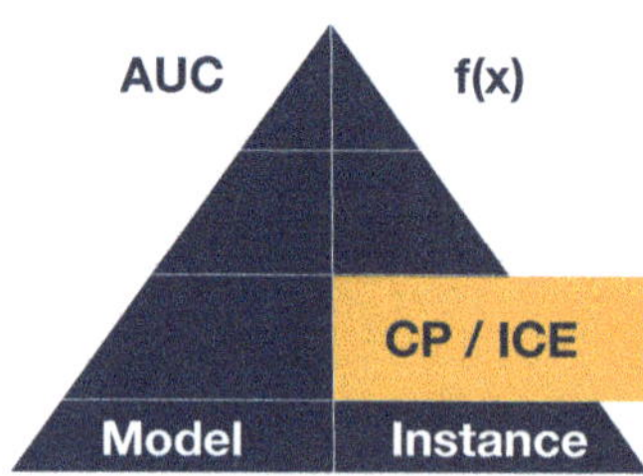

Ceteris Paribus

Ceteris Paribus (CP) is a Latin phrase for "other things being equal". It is also a very useful technique for an analysis of model behaviour for a single observation. CP profiles, sometimes called Individual Conditional Expectations (ICE), show how the model response would change for a selected observation if a value for one variable was changed while leaving the other variables unchanged.

While local variable attribution is a convenient technique for answering the question of **which** variables affect the prediction, the local profile analysis is a good technique for answering the question of **how** the model response depends on a particular variable. Or answering the question of **what if**...

R snippets

The `predict_profiles()` function calculates Ceteris Paribus profiles for a selected model and selected observations. By default, it calculates profiles for all variables, but one can limit this list with the `variables` vector of variables.

```
cp_ranger <- predict_profile(model_ranger, Steve)
cp_ranger
#  Top profiles    :
#        Gender    Age Cardiovascular.Diseases Diabetes
# 1      Female 76.00                      Yes       No
# 1.1      Male 76.00                      Yes       No
# 11       Male  0.00                      Yes       No
# 1.110    Male  0.99                      Yes       No
```

The calculated profiles can be drawn with the generic `plot` function. As with other explanations in the `DALEX` library, multiple models can be plotted on a single graph. Although for technical reasons quantitative and qualitative variables cannot be shown in a single chart. So if you want to show the importance of quality variables, you need to plot them separately.

Figure 23 shows an example of a CP profile for continuous variable `Age` and categorical variable `Cardiovascular.Diseases`.

```
# See Figure 23
plot(cp_ranger, variables = "Age")
plot(cp_ranger, variables = "Cardiovascular.Diseases",
         categorical_type = "lines")
```

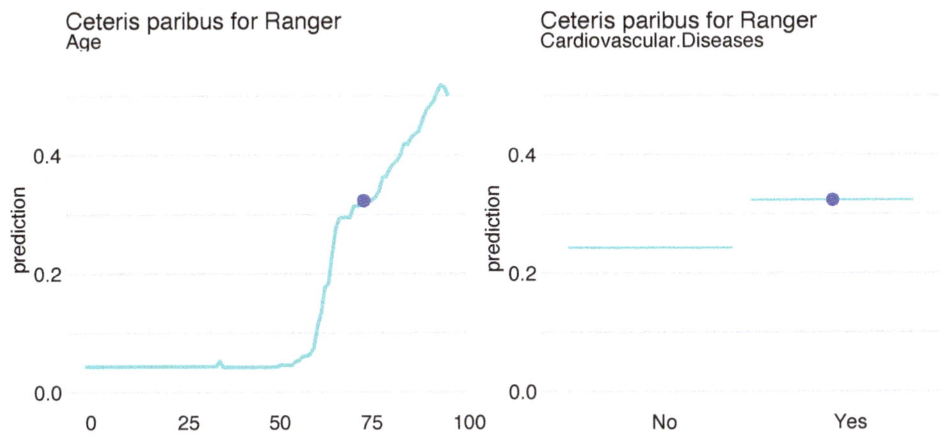

Figure 23: The dot shows the observation under analysis. CP profile shows how the model predictions change for changes in the selected variable. On the left is the CP profile for the continuous variable `Age`, on the right for the categorical variable `Cardiovascular.Diseases`. For categorical variables, one can specify how the CP profiles should be drawn by setting the `categorical_type` argument.

The `plot` function can combine multiple models, making it easier to see similarities and differences.

```
cp_cdc <- predict_profile(model_cdc, Steve)
cp_tree <- predict_profile(model_tree, Steve)
cp_tune <- predict_profile(model_tuned, Steve)
# See Figure 24
plot(cp_cdc, cp_tree, cp_ranger, cp_tune, variables = "Age")
```

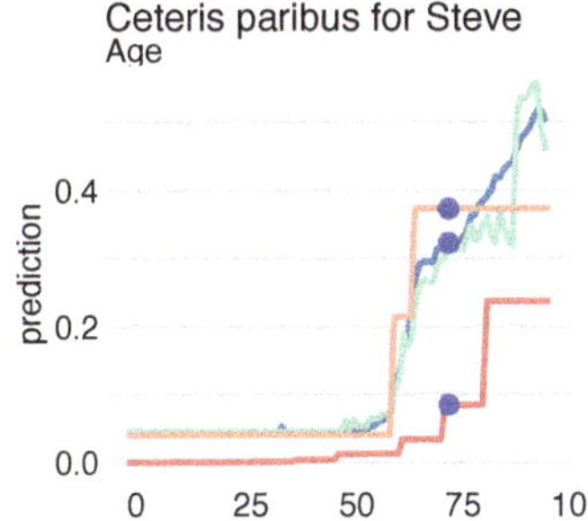

Figure 24: CP profiles for Steve, colors code four considered models.

CP profiles are also useful for finding the importance of variables in a model. The more the profiles fluctuate, the more influential the variable is. Such a measure of importance is implemented in the `predict_parts` function under option `type = "oscillations"`[40].

```
predict_parts(model_ranger, Steve, type = "oscillations")
#                     _vname_ _ids_  oscillations
# 2                       Age     1    0.22872998
# 6           Kidney.Diseases     1    0.16371903
# 7                    Cancer     1    0.09641507
# 4                  Diabetes     1    0.05052652
# 3   Cardiovascular.Diseases     1    0.03984208
# 1                    Gender     1    0.03308303
# 5     Neurological.Diseases     1    0.03164090
```

[40] The size of the oscillation can be measured in many ways, by default, it is an area between the CP profile and a horizontal line at the level of the model prediction.

HERE WE HAVE A DETAILED RISK ANALYSIS FOR STEVE.
HIS HIGH SCORE MOSTLY RESULTS FROM AGE AND HYPERTENSION. THE OTHER CHARACTERISTICS CHANGE VIRTUALLY LITTLE.
IMIĘ: STEVE
NAZWISKO: S.
WIEK: 76 LAT
PŁEĆ: M
CHOROBY: NADCIŚNIENIE
Intercept
Age = 76
Cardiovascu... ...es = Yes
Gender = Male
Cancer = No
Kidney Diseases = No
Neurological Diseases = No
Diabetes = No
prediction
0.043
+0.181
0.268
THE RISK INCREASES WITH AGE. AFTER AGE 60, WE SEE A STEEP RISE IN THE GRAPH.
Ceteris Paribus profile
created for the AutoTune model
Age
prediction
STEVE NEEDS TO BE VACCINATED QUICKLY.

IT IS NOW THAT WE CAN CALCULATE EACH PERSON'S INDIVIDUAL RISK.
AND HAVING THAT, PRECISELY PLAN THE ORDER IN WHICH AGENTS ARE VACCINATED.
HERE WE HAVE A LIST OF AGENTS.
I'LL PREPARE AN APP.
WE WILL MAKE IT AVAILABLE ON PAGE CRS19.PL
SO THAT EVERYONE CAN CALCULATE THEIR INDIVIDUAL RISK ASSESSMENT.
WE'LL PREPARE A REPORT.
AND AS WE DO, WE WILL SEND IT AT THE LAST MINUTE, BUT WITHIN THE TIME LIMITS SET BY MR. MI2.
KLIK!
Covid-19 risk calculator
Explain risk of:
Severe condition
Death
Gender: female, Age: 76, Cardiovascular Disease
After diagnosis of Covid-19 disease, the conditional probability of
severe condition is 17.9%
death is 14.72%
Cardiovascular Disease
Cancer
Explain severe condition prediction
What if age will change

Model Deployment

We have made the model built for Covid data, along with the explanations described in this book, available at `https://crs19.pl/` webpage. After two months, tens of thousands of people used it. With proper tools the deployment of such a model is not difficult.

To obtain a safe and effective model, it is necessary to perform a detailed Explanatory Model Analysis. However, we often don't have much time for it. That is why tools that facilitate fast and automated model exploration are so useful.

One of such tools is `modelStudio`[41]. It is a package that transforms an explainer into an HTML page with javascript based interaction. Such an HTML page is easy to save on a disk or share by email. The webpage has various explanations pre-calculated, so its generation may be time-consuming, but the model exploration is very fast, and the feedback loop is tight.

Generating a `modelStudio` for an explainer is trivially easy.

[41] Hubert Baniecki and Przemyslaw Biecek. The Grammar of Interactive Explanatory Model Analysis. *Arxiv*, 2020. URL `https://arxiv.org/abs/2005.00497`

```
library("modelStudio")
ms <- modelStudio(model_ranger)
# See Figure 25
ms
```

Figure 25: modelStudio is an application that facilitates model exploration using a serverless site based on javascript. The user can configure the content of each panel to look at the model from different perspectives.

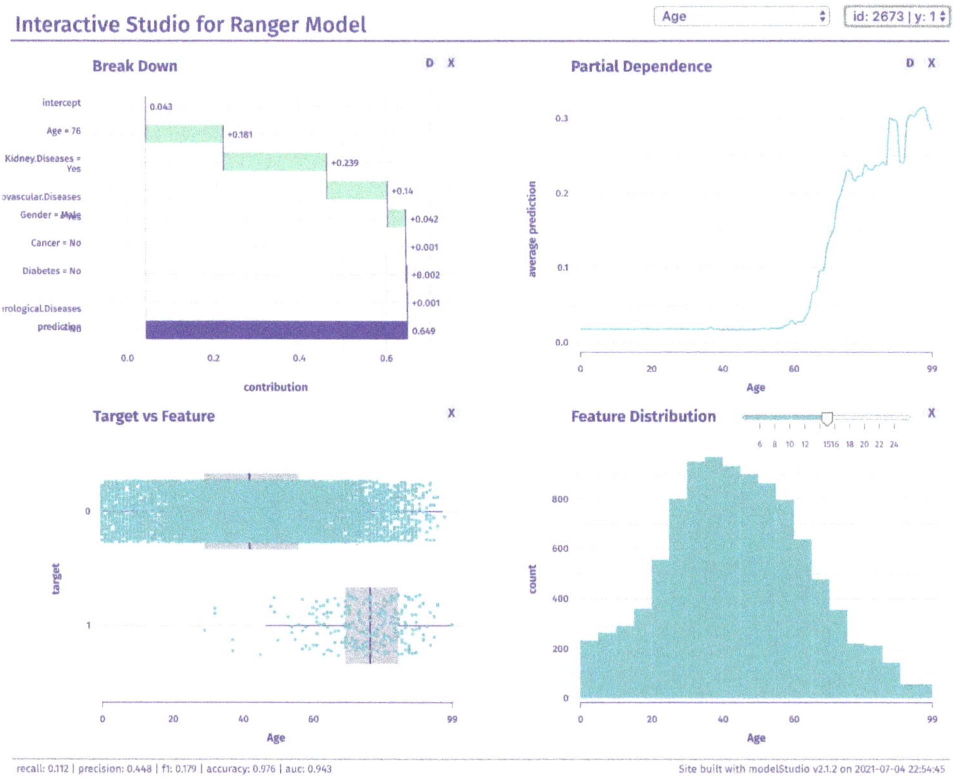

An example dashboard built for a model for dozens of variables and several thousand rows on football player worth prediction based on the FIFA dataset is available at

`https://pbiecek.github.io/explainFIFA20/`.

If we want to automate comparison of several models, `Arena` is a very convenient tool for such exploration. It can work in two modes: live (with the server which adds the necessary statistics on the fly) or pre-calculated statistics. In the case of many models and large datasets, the live mode is much more convenient.

The dashboard is created with the `create_arena` function. Then with `push_model` and `push_observations`, one can add more models and more observations for model exploration. The resulting object can be turned into the live web application with the `run_server` function.

The snippet below turns four covid models into a dashboard.

```r
library("arenar")
library("dplyr")

covid_ar <- create_arena(live = TRUE) %>%
    push_model(model_cdc) %>%
    push_model(model_tree) %>%
    push_model(model_ranger) %>%
    push_model(model_tuned) %>%
    push_observations(Steve)
# See Figure 26
run_server(covid_ar)
```

Figure 26: The `arenar` is a web application that facilitates exploration of multiple models.

An example dashboard built for a model for dozens of variables and several thousand rows on football player worth prediction based on the FIFA dataset is available at `https://arena.drwhy.ai/?demo=1`.

I'LL SAY IT NOW. IT'S OVER!
AND I WILL AGREE WITH YOU THIS TIME.
IT WAS A CHALLENGING TASK. NOW WE ARE FREE. LET'S DO SOMETHING CRAZY.
TWO MINUTES LATER...
???

Come on, sister. You're the one with the idea of fun.
Programming AI to play Tetri, this is something.
Explain Explain Explain
... BETAAA!!!
How about thinking about where you can use similar models?
MI DATA LAB

The Hitchhiker's Guide to Responsible Machine Learning

The R version

Authors:
Przemysław Biecek, Anna Kozak, Aleksander Zawada

Illustrations and cover:
Aleksander Zawada

Reviewer:
Łukasz Rajkowski

Proofreading:
Bożena Przybyła

Free flipbook:
`https://betaandbit.github.io/RML/`

Buy pdf online:
`https://leanpub.com/RML`

Data and reproducible code snippets:
`https://github.com/BetaAndBit/RML`

Publisher:
Scientific Foundation SmarterPoland.pl

ISBN:
978-83-65291-12-7

Edition I
Warsaw 2022